COLLECTORS' SERIES

Masters of the Dark Art

VOL. 2: STEVEN J. BEJMA

ASYLUM

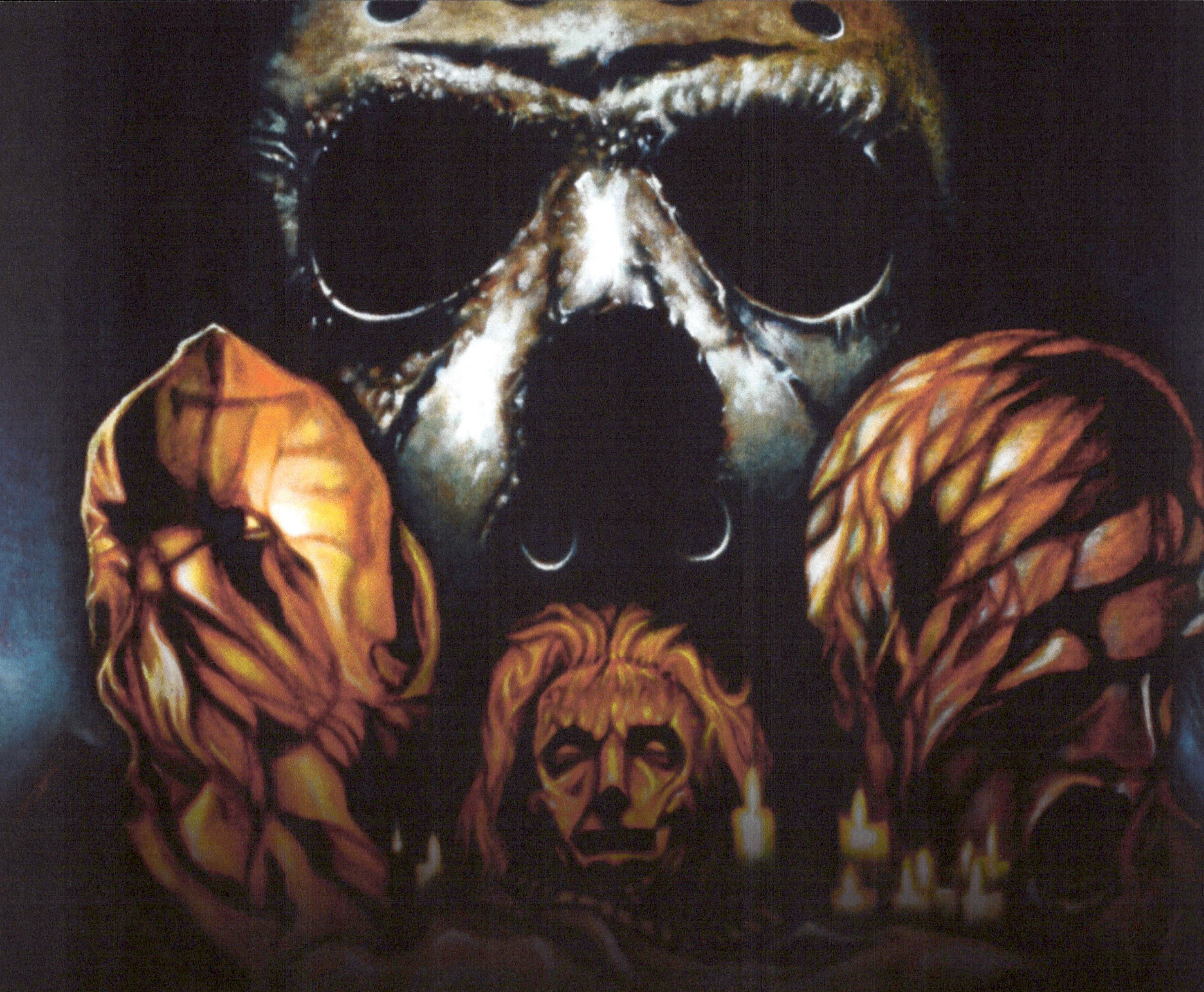

ARTWORK BY STEVEN J. BEJMA
EDITED BY JOSHUA WERNER & PAUL BURKE

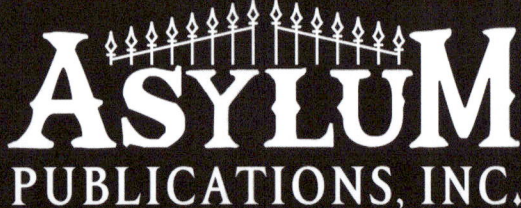

Distributed by

CEO AND EDITOR IN CHIEF PAUL BURKE
CREATIVE DIRECTOR JOSHUA WERNER

ISBN: 978-1-7339309-5-6

Masters of the Dark Art Vol. 2: Steven J. Bejma™. Published by Asylum Publications, Inc.™ All images are © by Steven J. Bejma. Asylum Pulications, Inc.™ and Masters of the Dark Art™ areTM 2019. All rights reserved. No portion of this publication may be reproduced or transmitted, in any form by any means, without written consent from the Publisher, except for any small excerpts for the purpose of review. For further information regarding custom photo/art books, ordering wholesale, or other inquiries, please write to asylumpublications75@gmail.com.

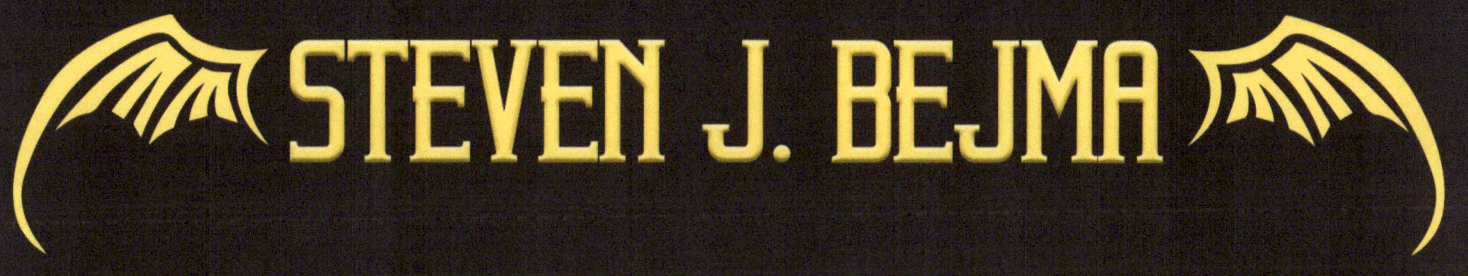

STEVEN J. BEJMA

I was born and raised in Michigan by a father who fostered a passion for all things creepy and scary. At an early age, I realized I had a talent for drawing while trying to copy the images I saw in the "Creepy and "Eerie" comics my dad and Aunt Mary Jane would smuggle to me at the chagrin of my mother.

My work is heavily influenced by the covers of those same comic artists such as Ken Kelly, Basil Gogos, and Frank Frazetta. It was their influence which drove me to teach myself to paint.

This book is dedicated to my dad, Ron Bejma, Sr. and my Aunt Mary Jane, without whose encouragement this book would not have been possible.

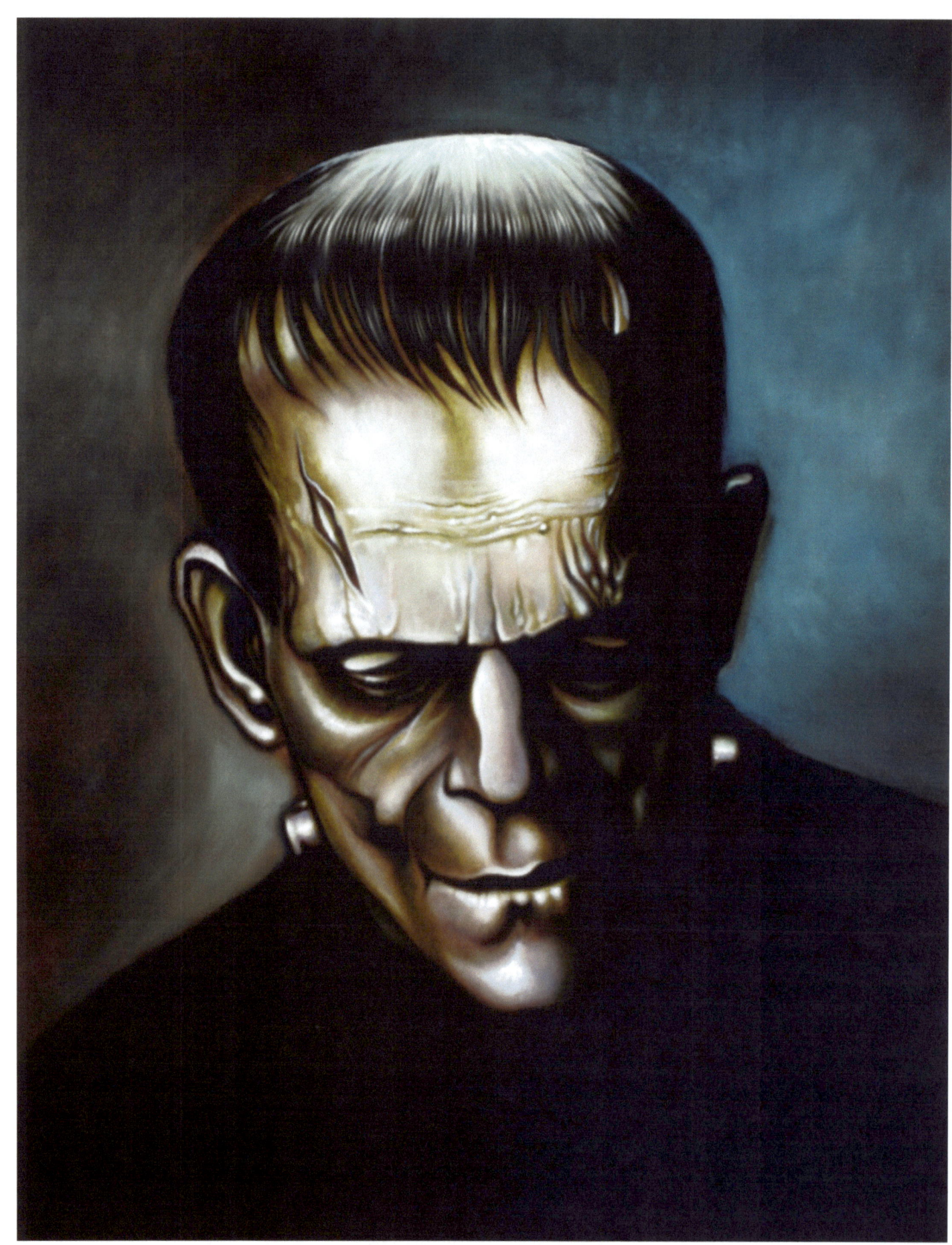

Frankenstein

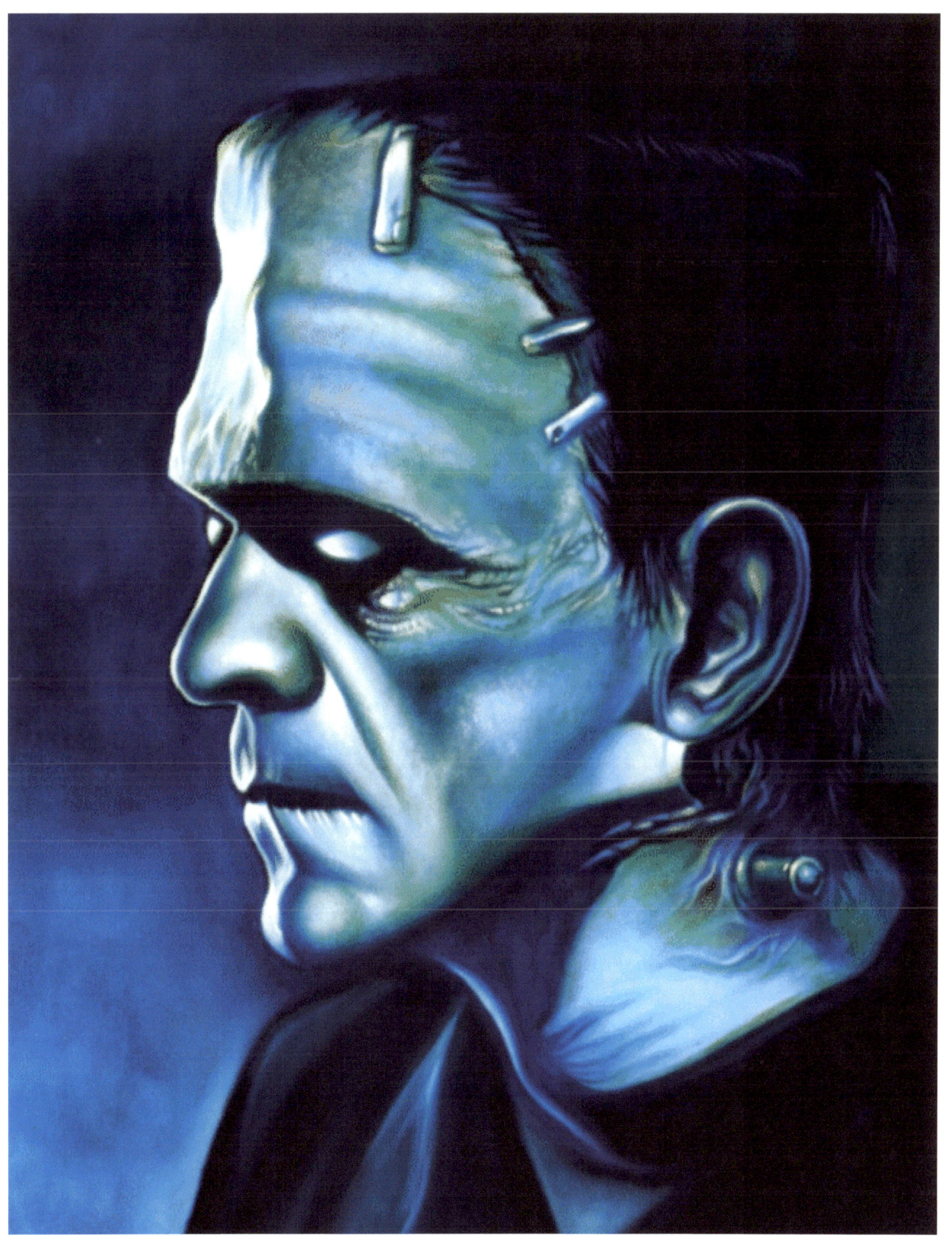

Frankenstein

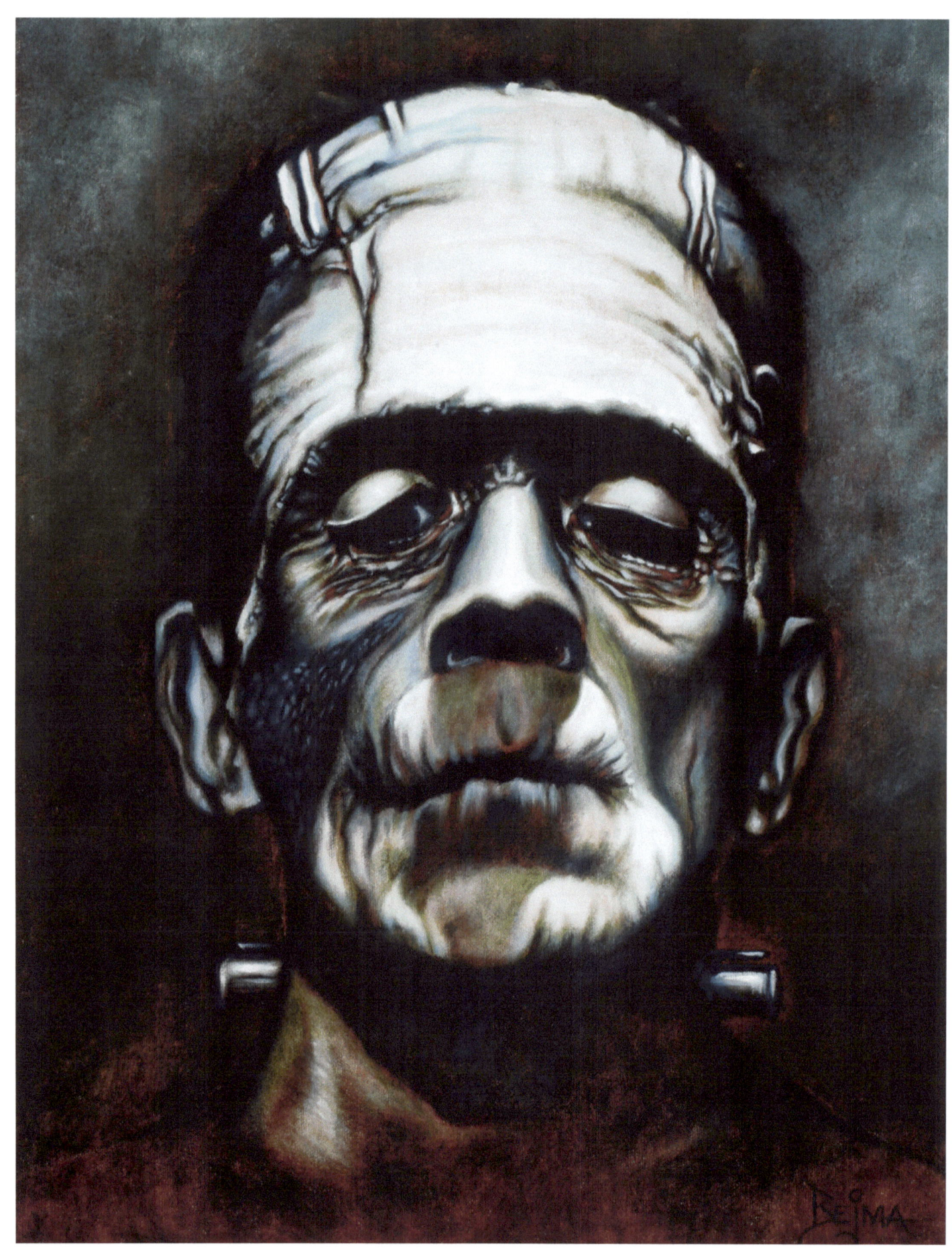

Frankenstein

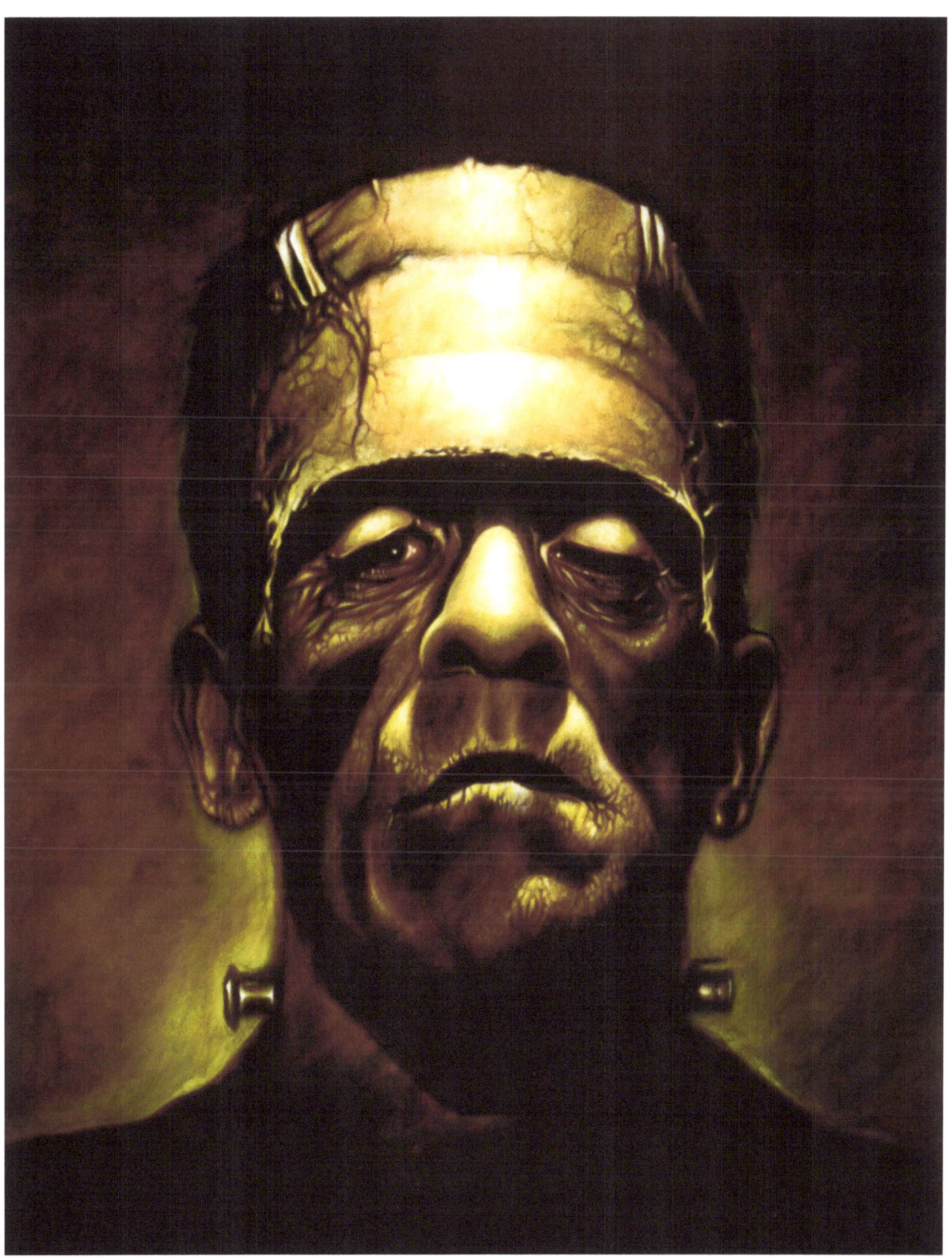

Frankenstein

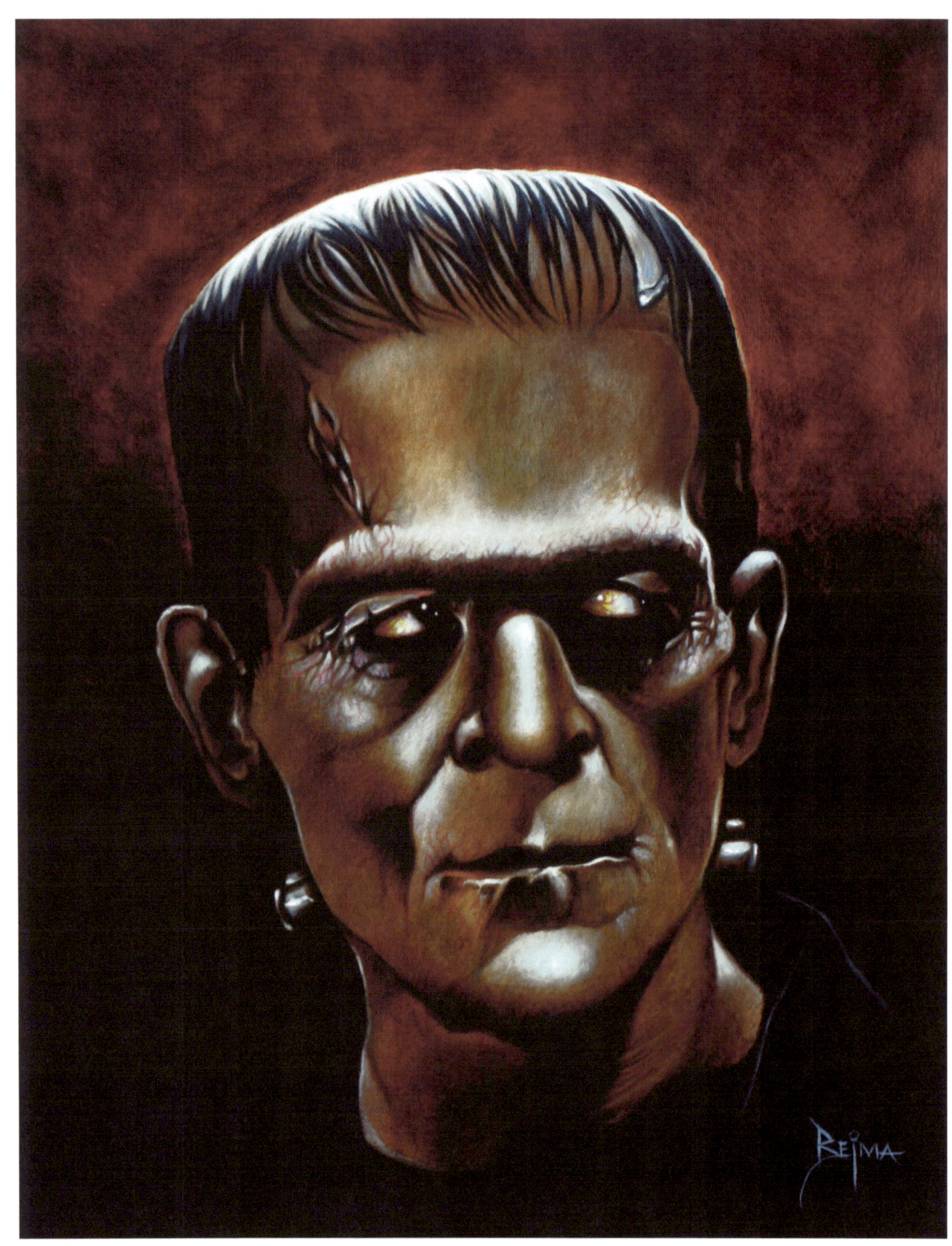

Frankenstein

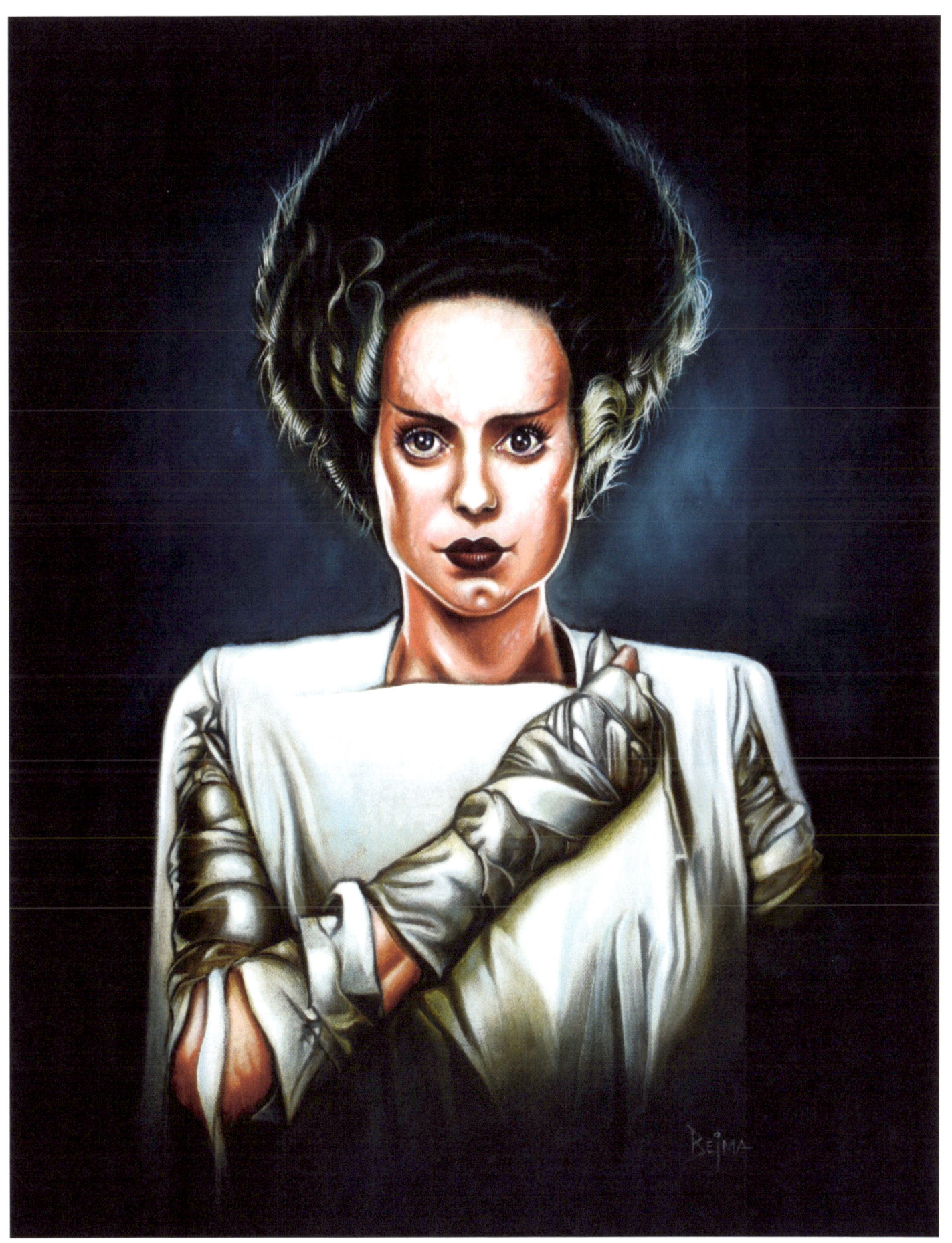

Bride of Frankenstein

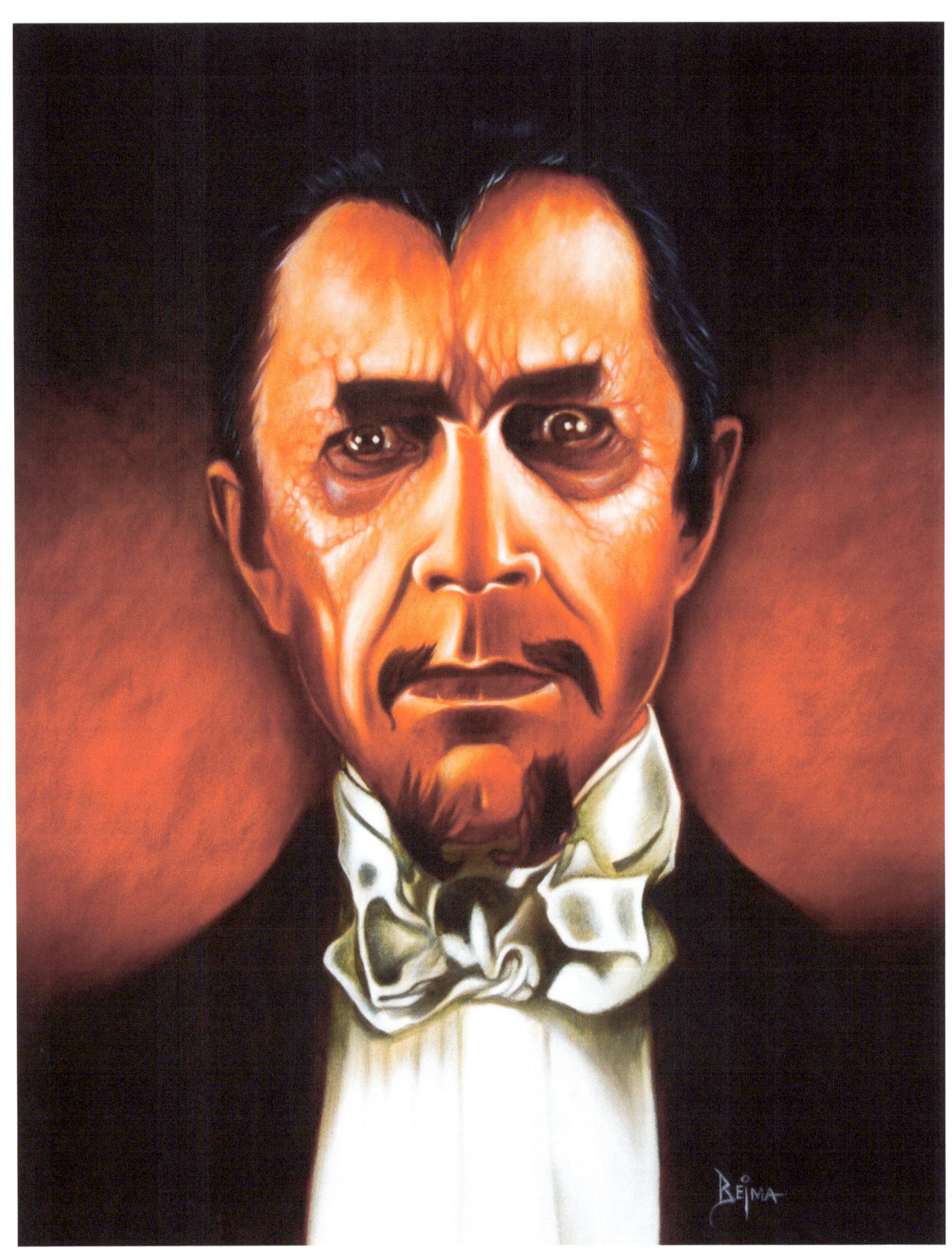

White Zombie

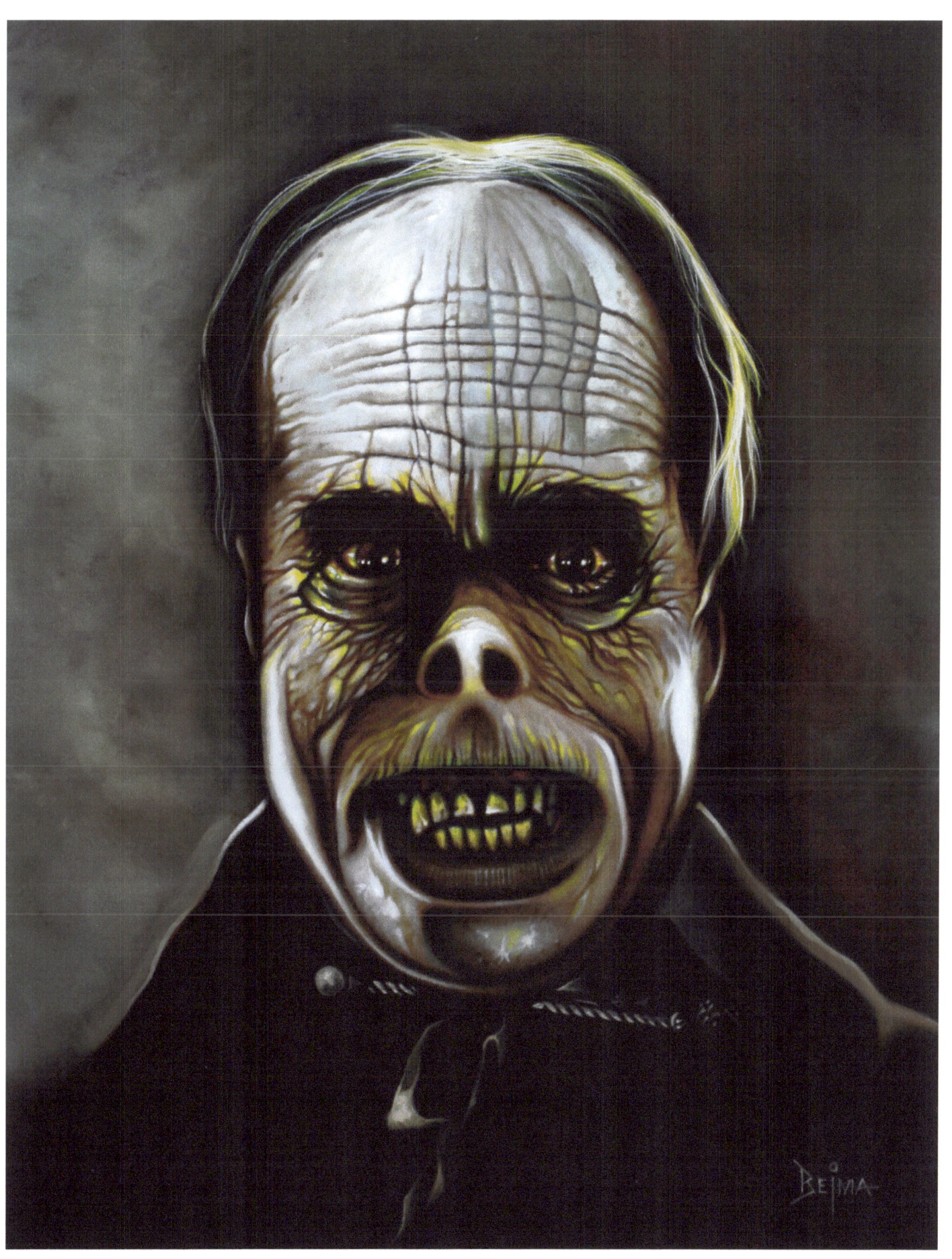

Phantom of the Opera

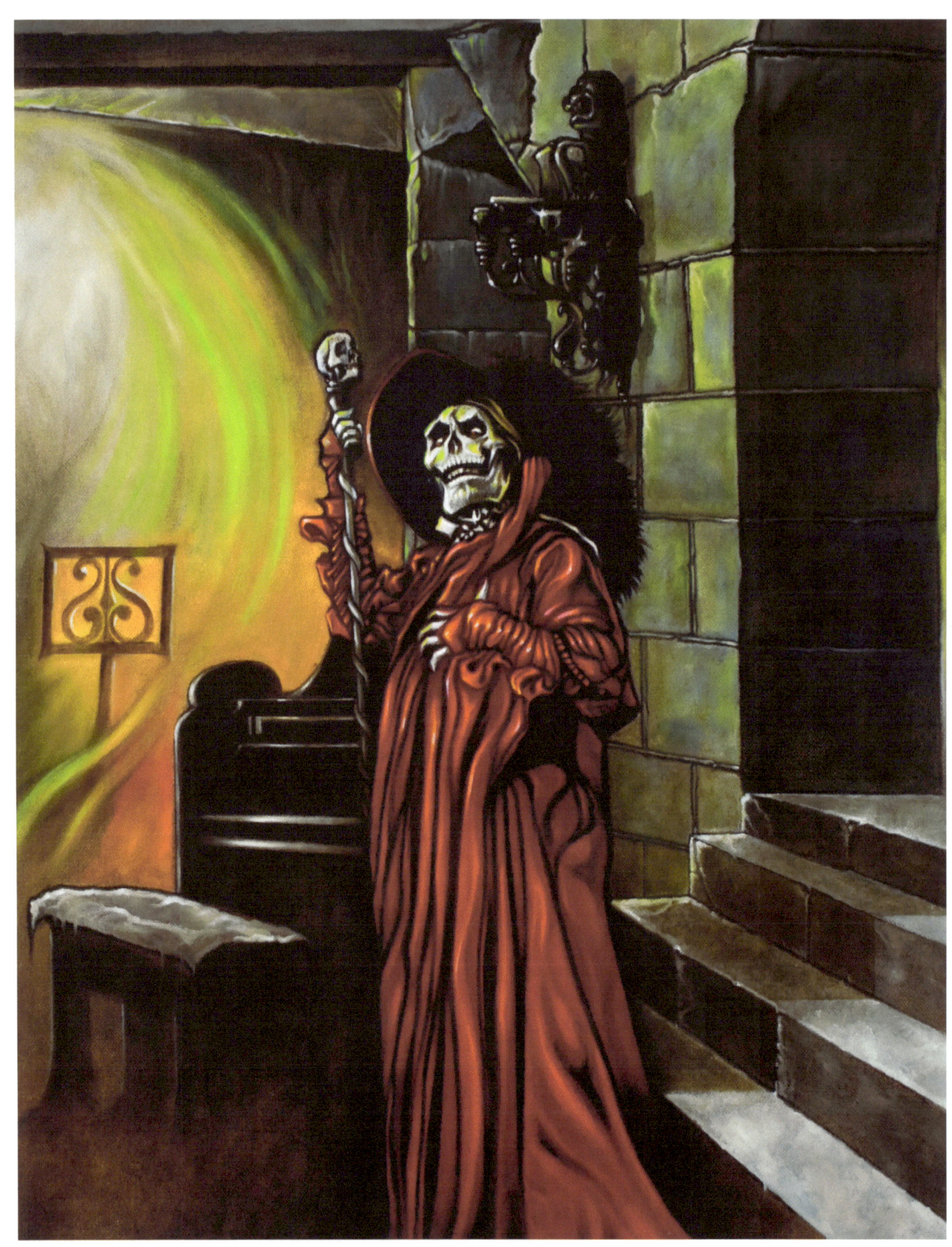

**Phantom of the Opera
For Scarlet Film Magazine**

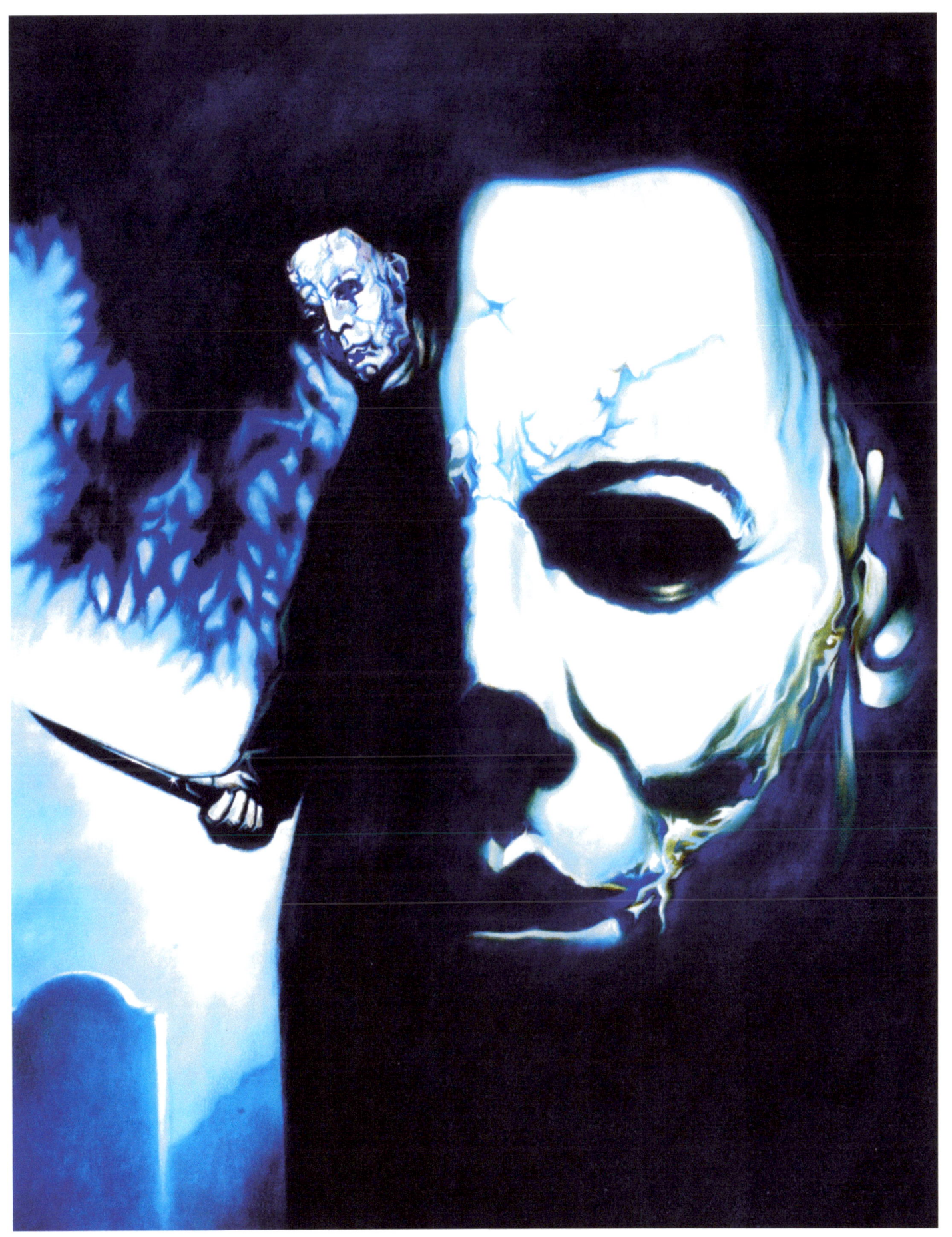

Halloween

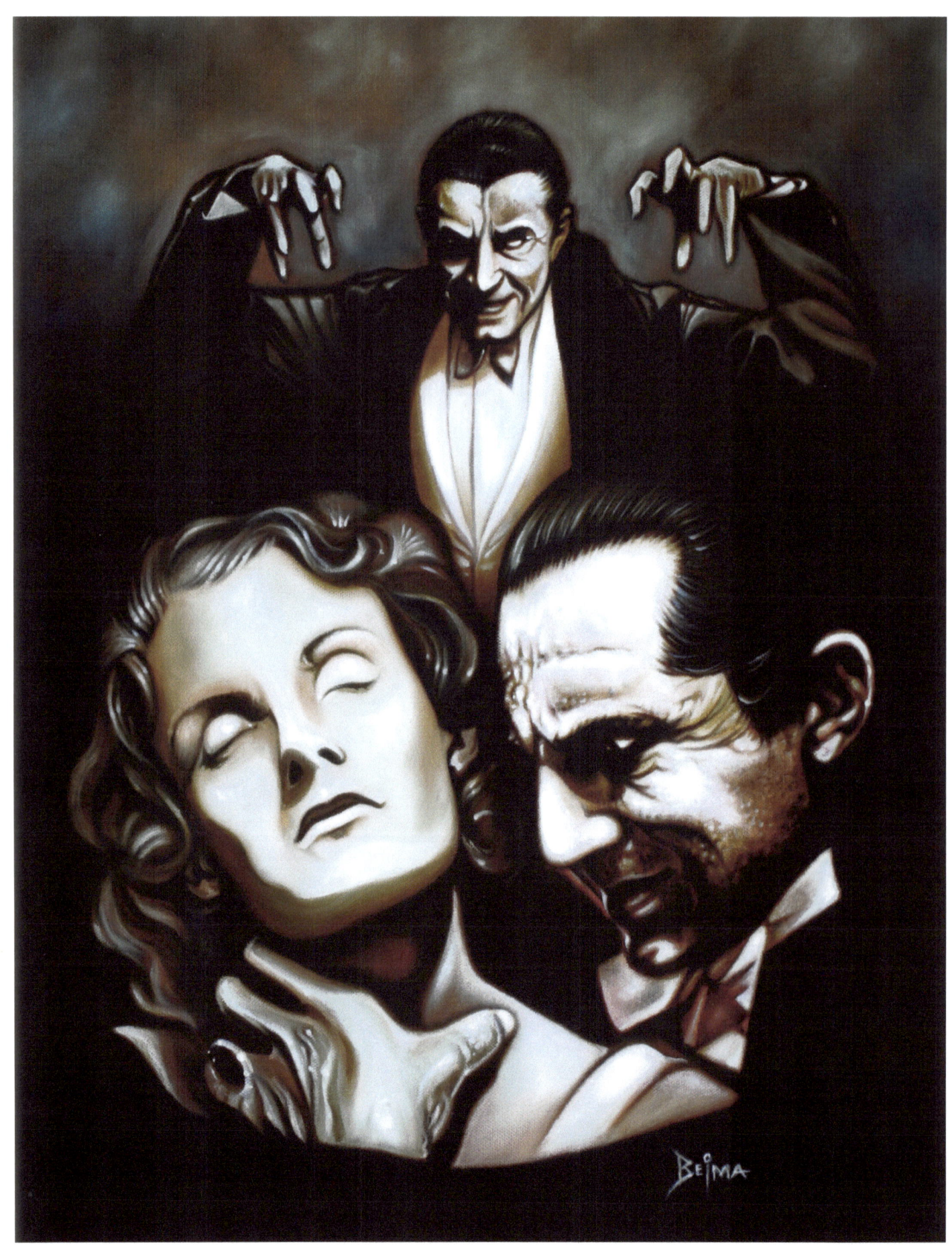

Dracula

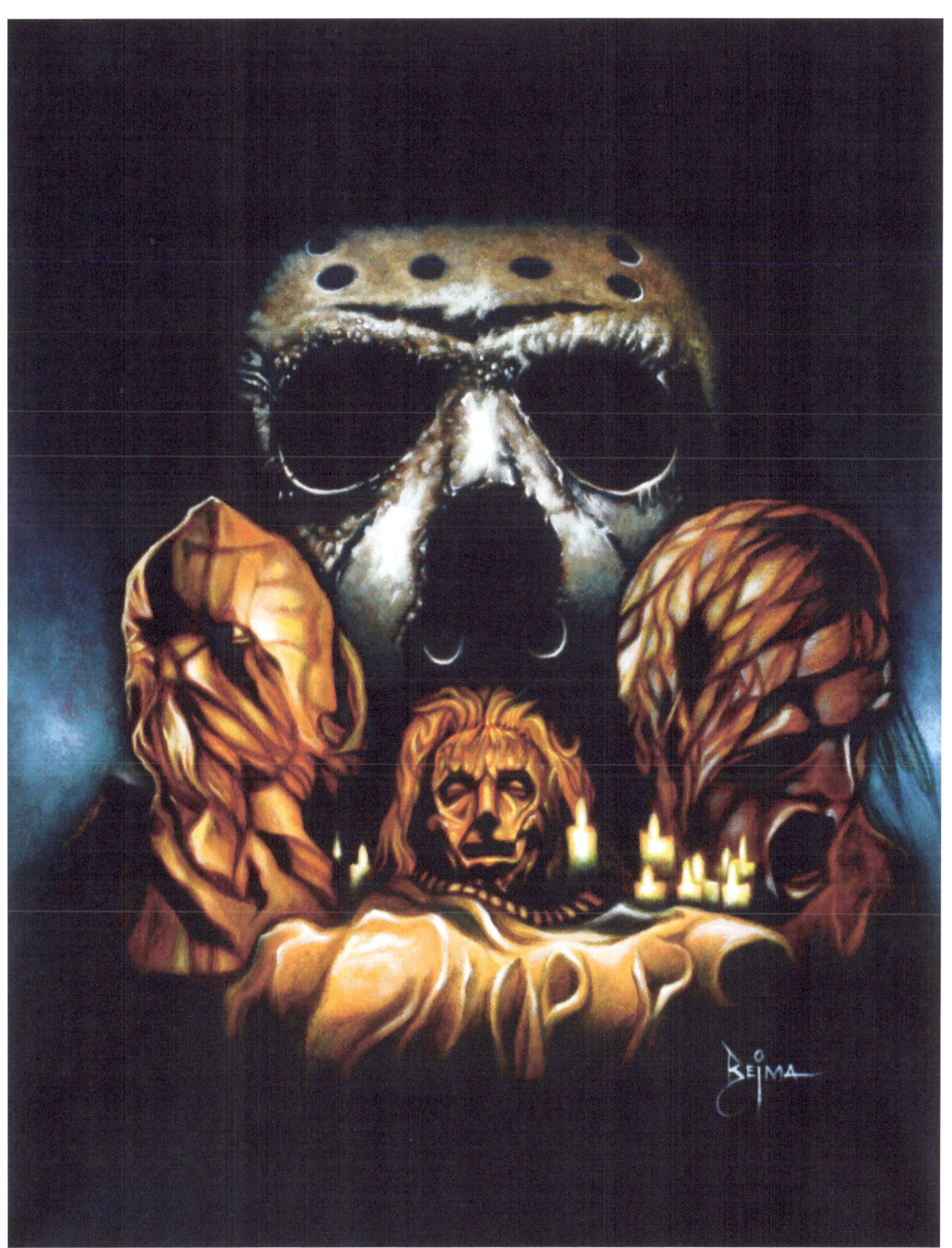

Friday the 13th

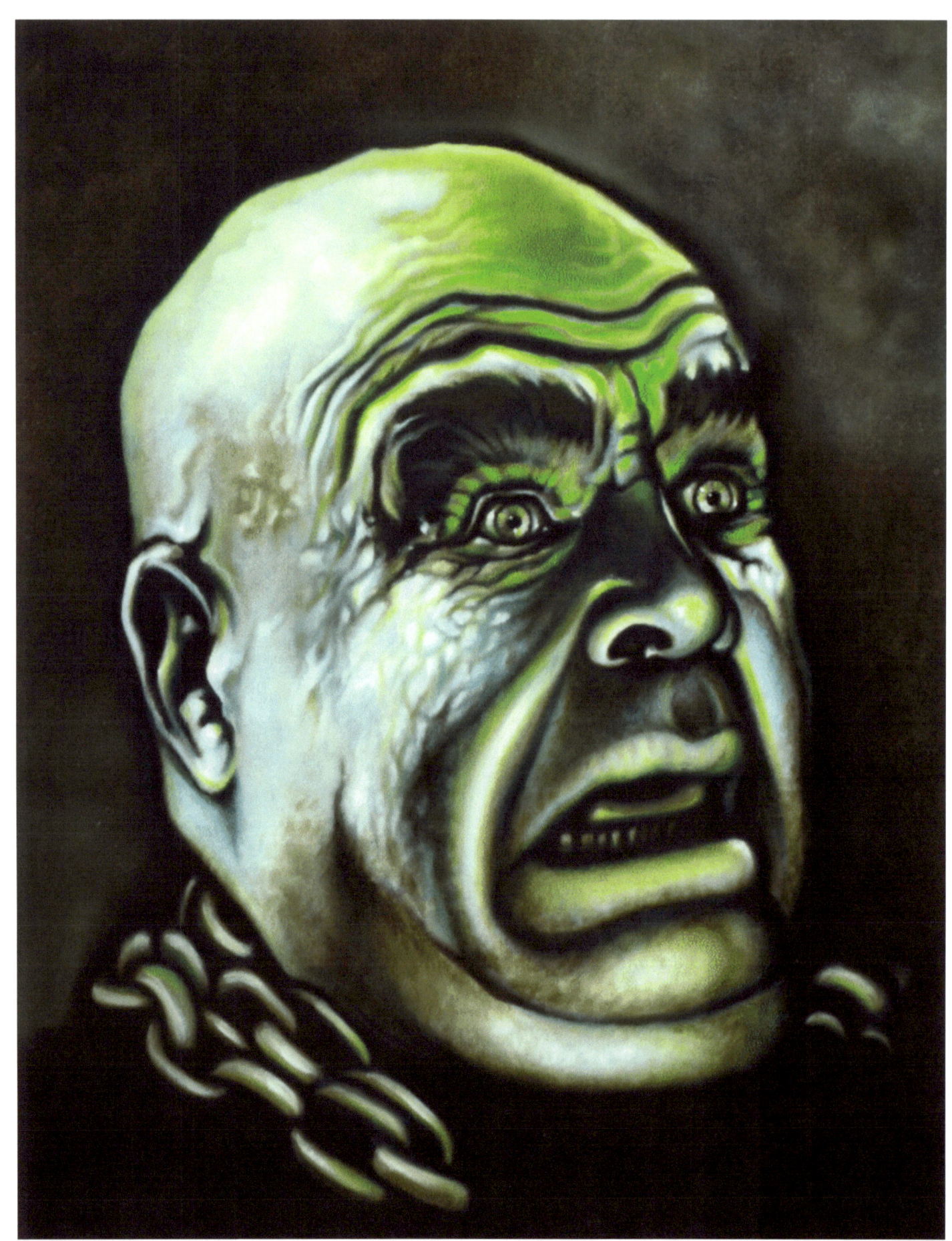

Tor Johnson

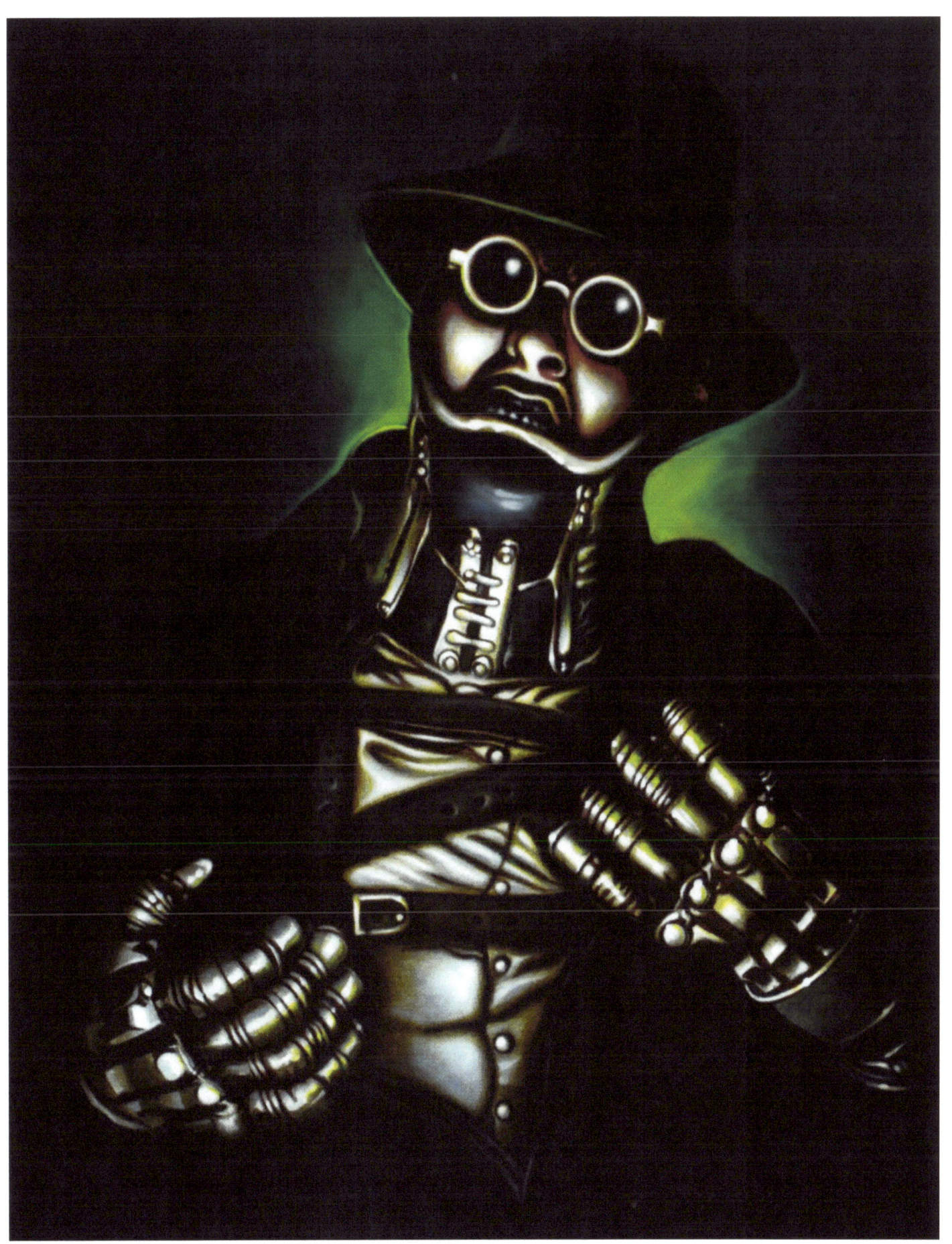

Mad Love

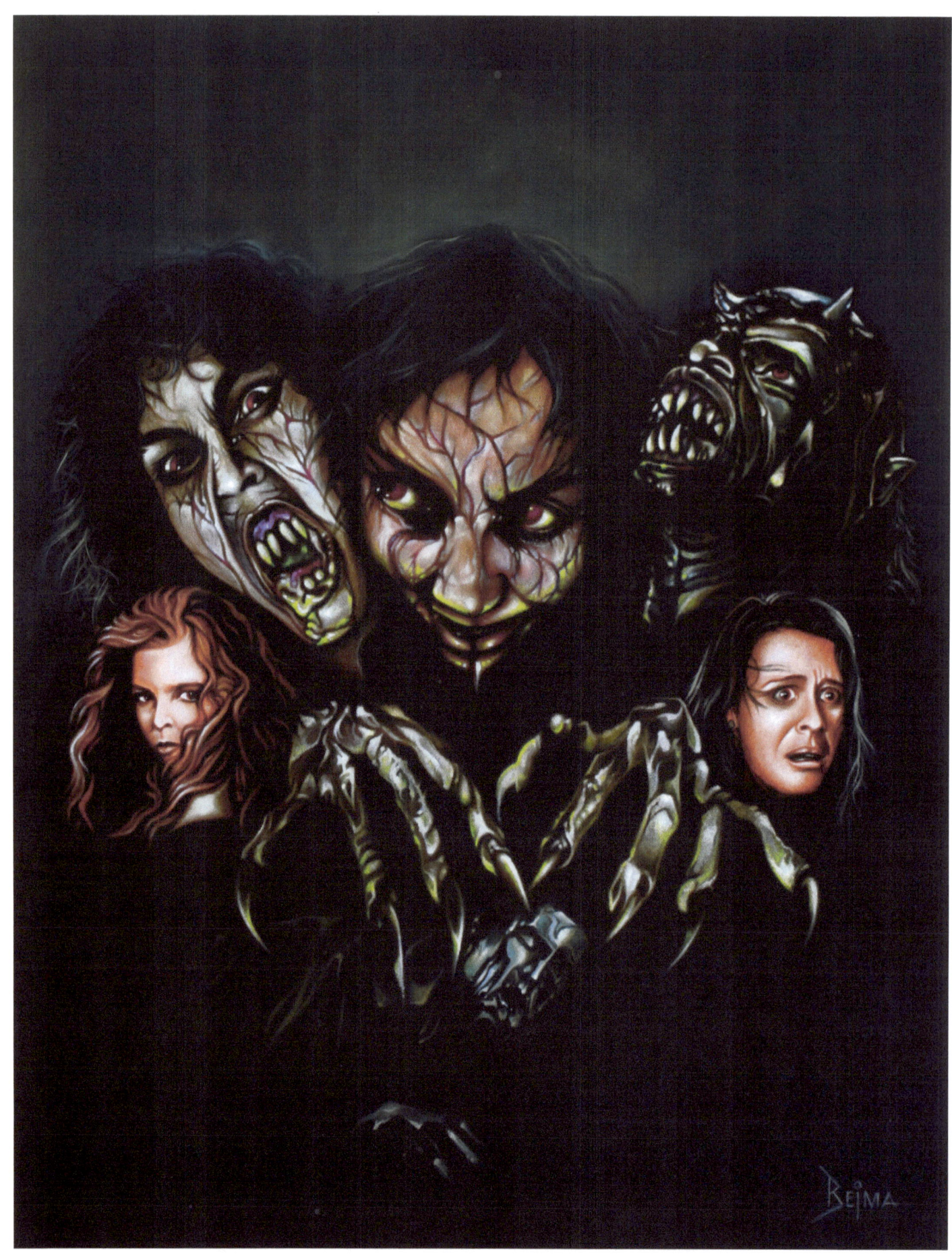

Demons

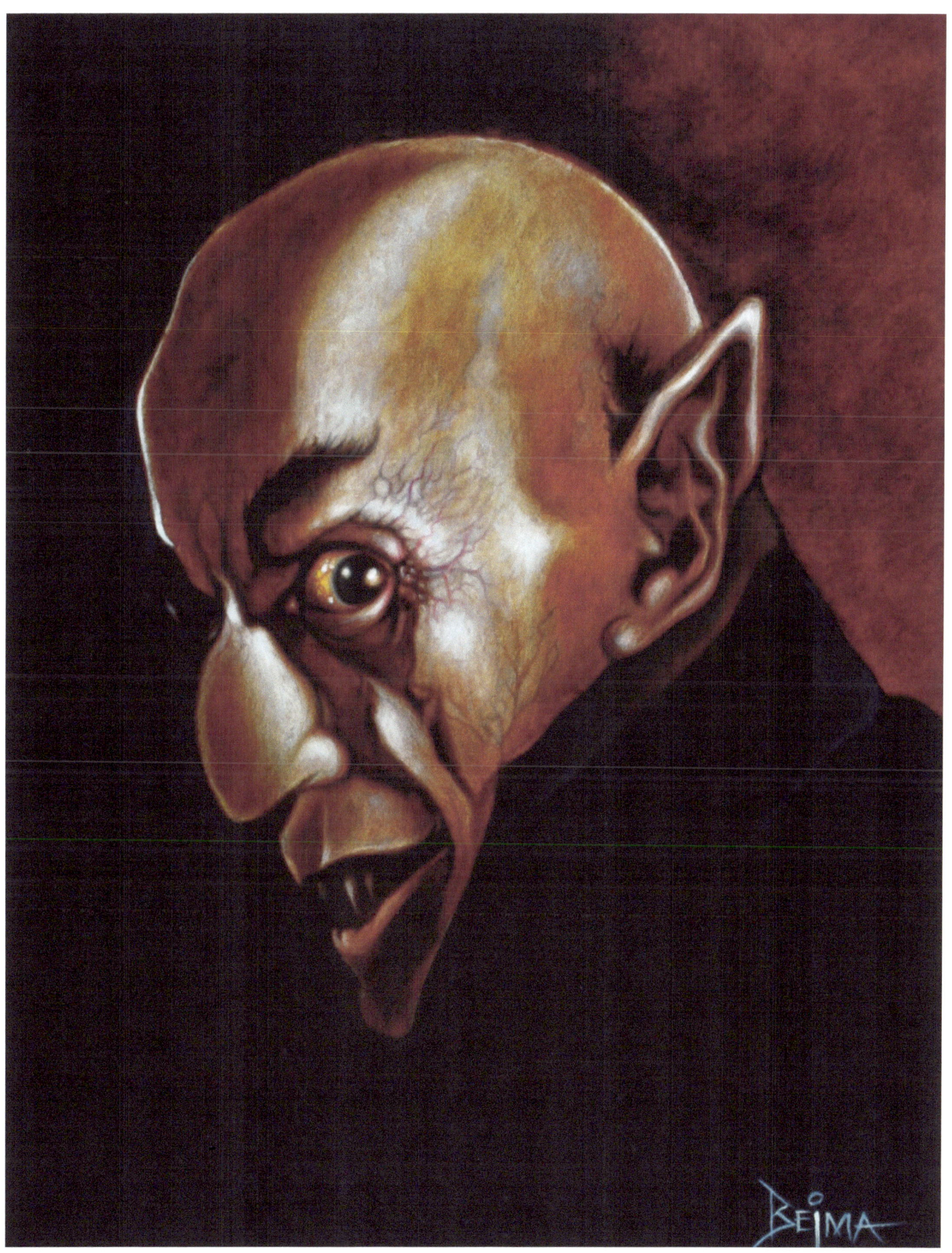

Nosferatu

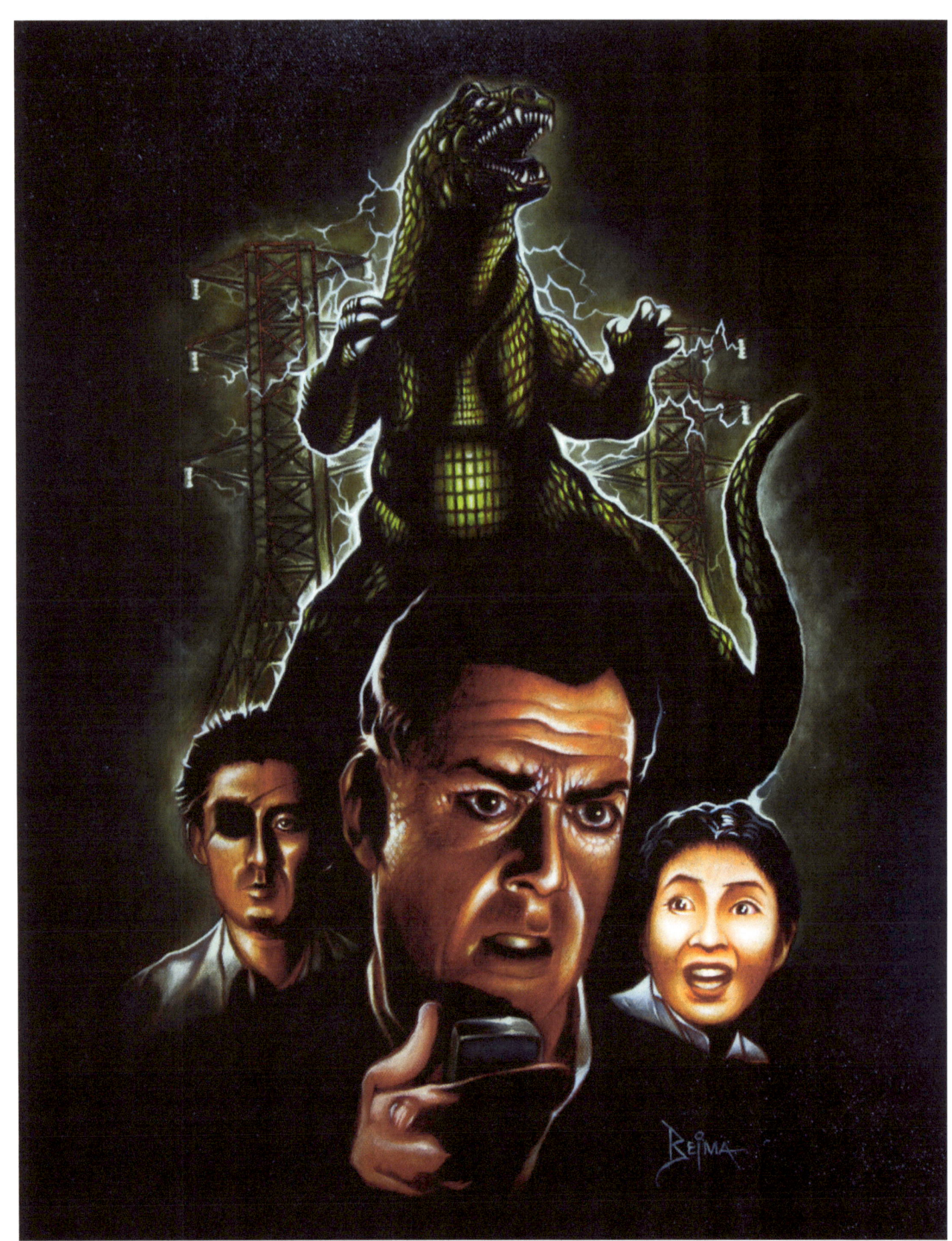

Godzilla

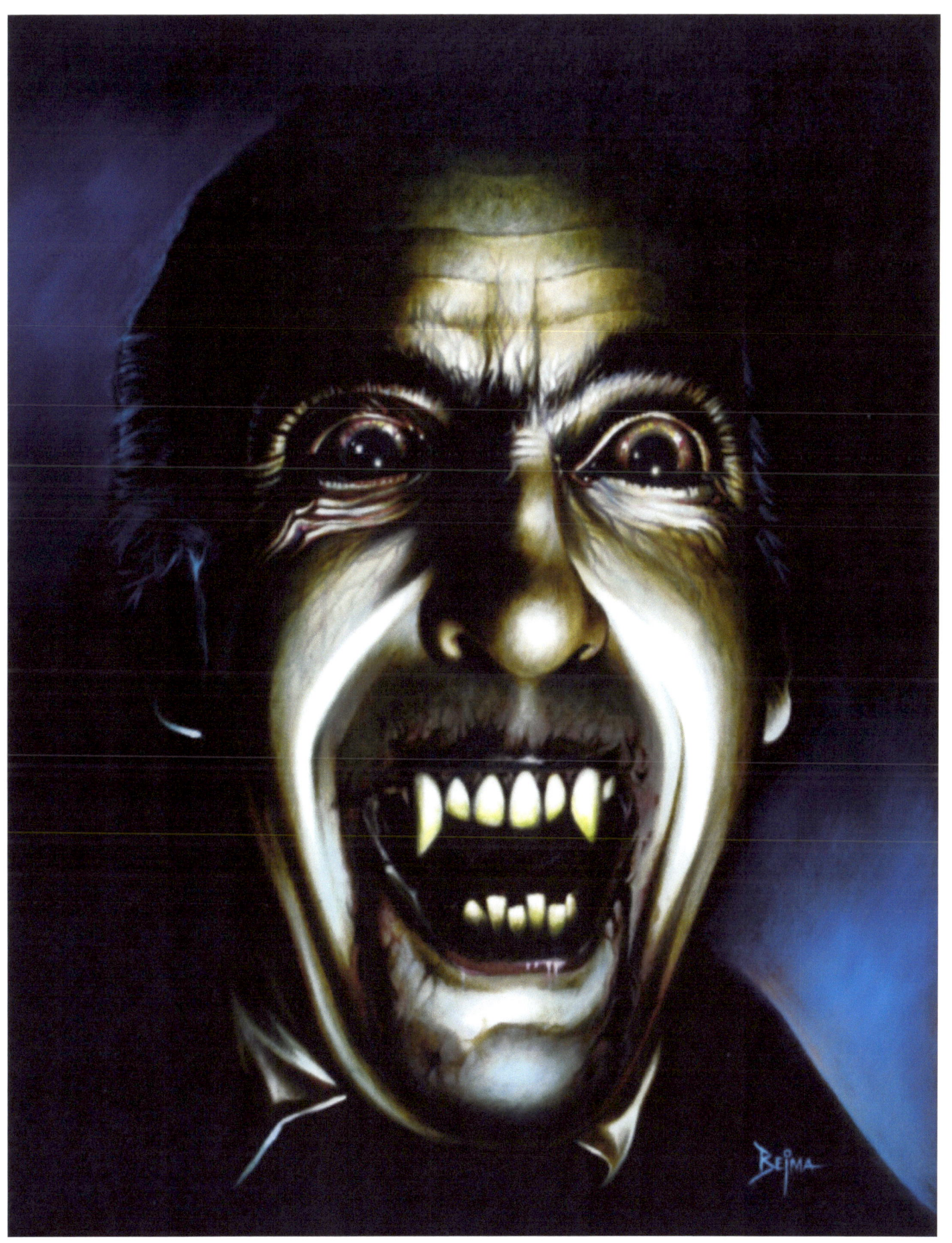

Horror of Dracula

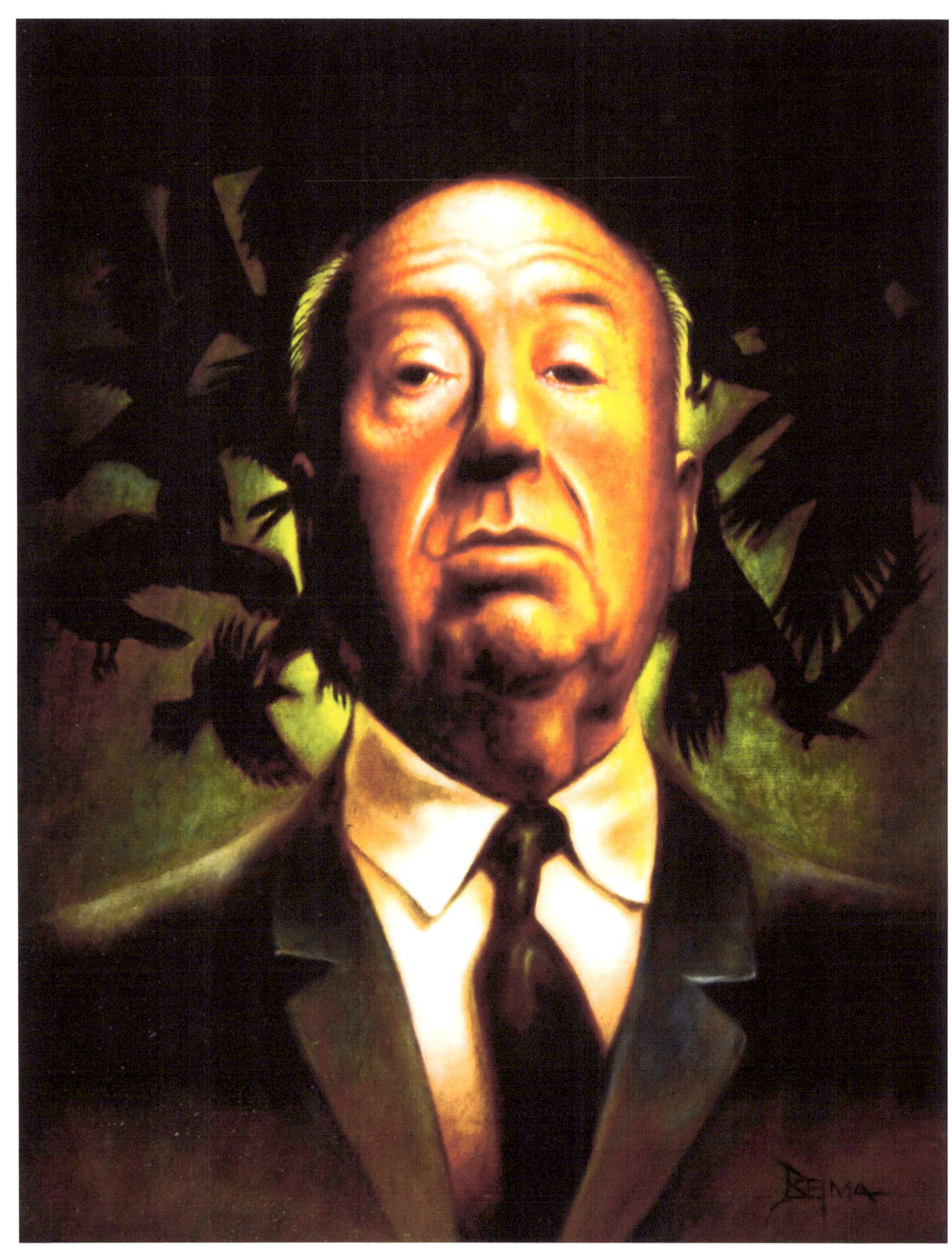

Alfred Hitchcock

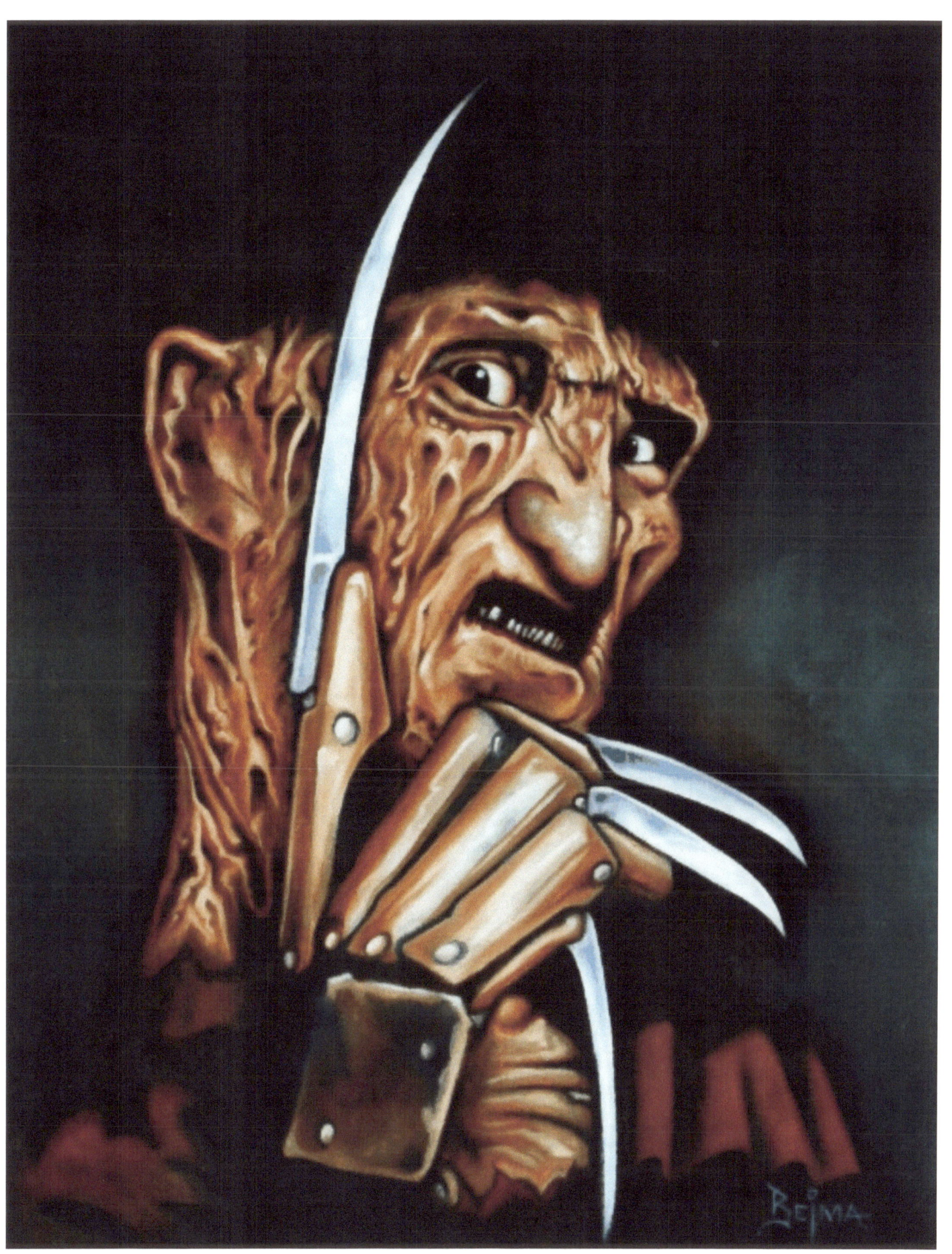

Nightmare on Elm Street

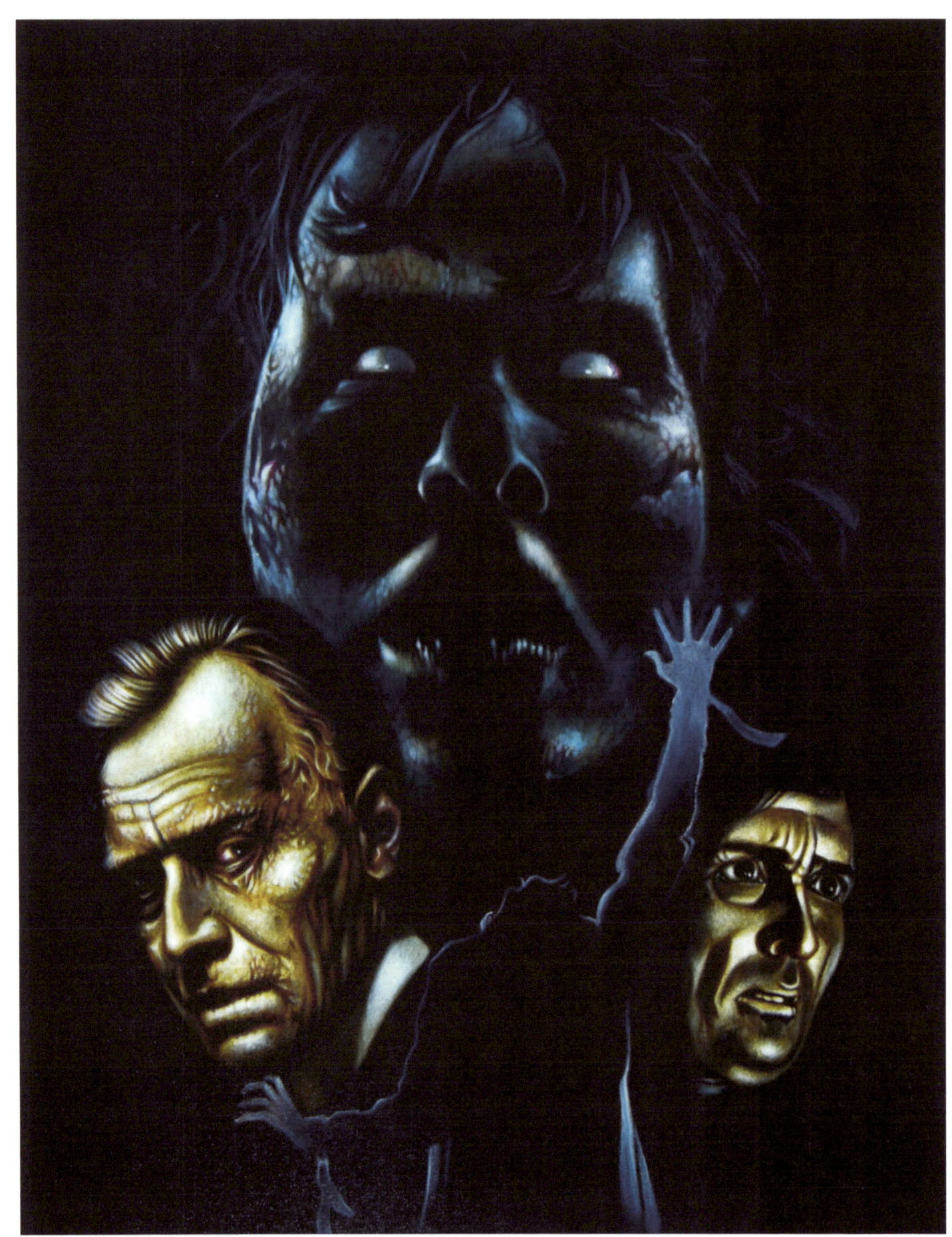

The Exorcist

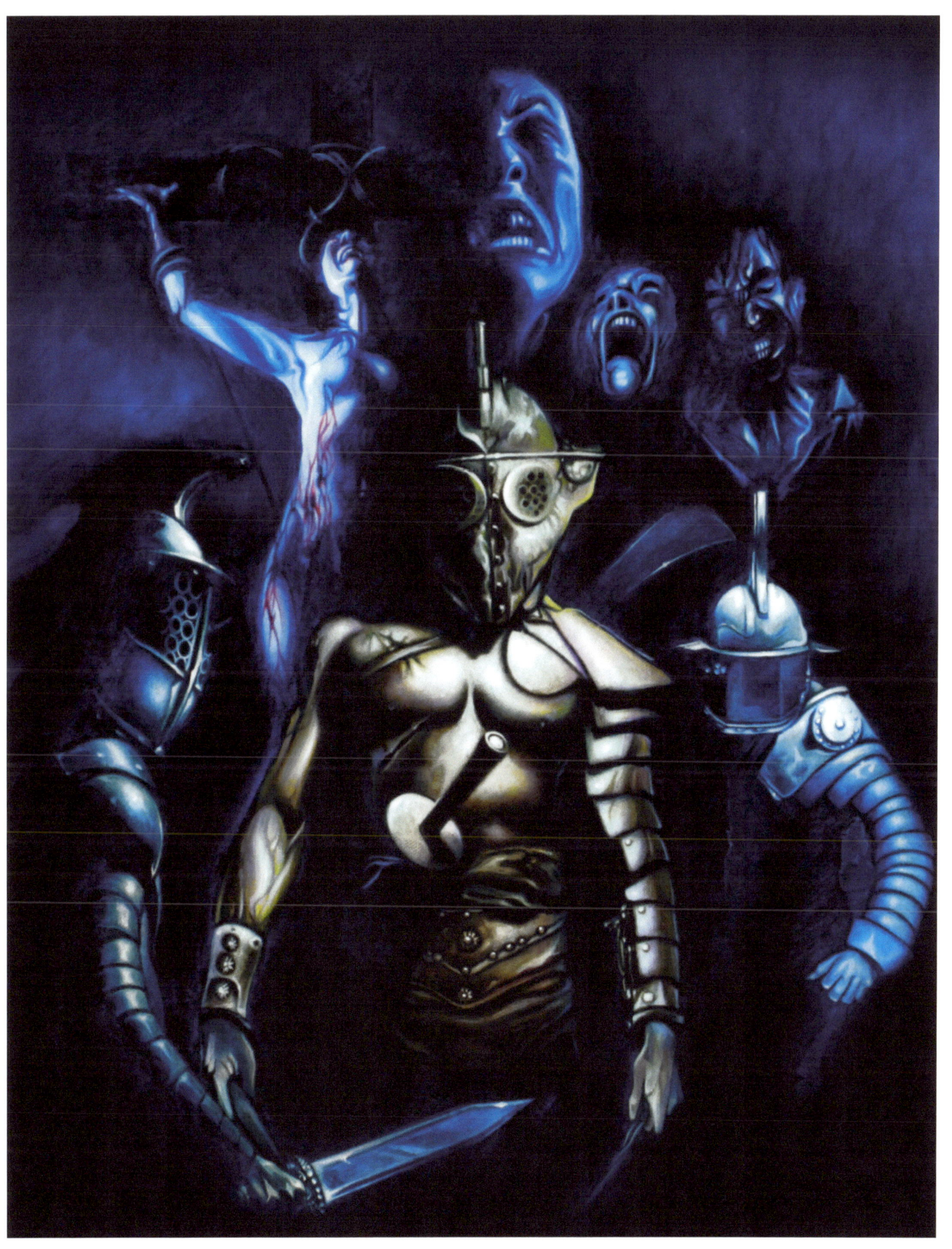

Morituros
DVD Cover for Synapse Films

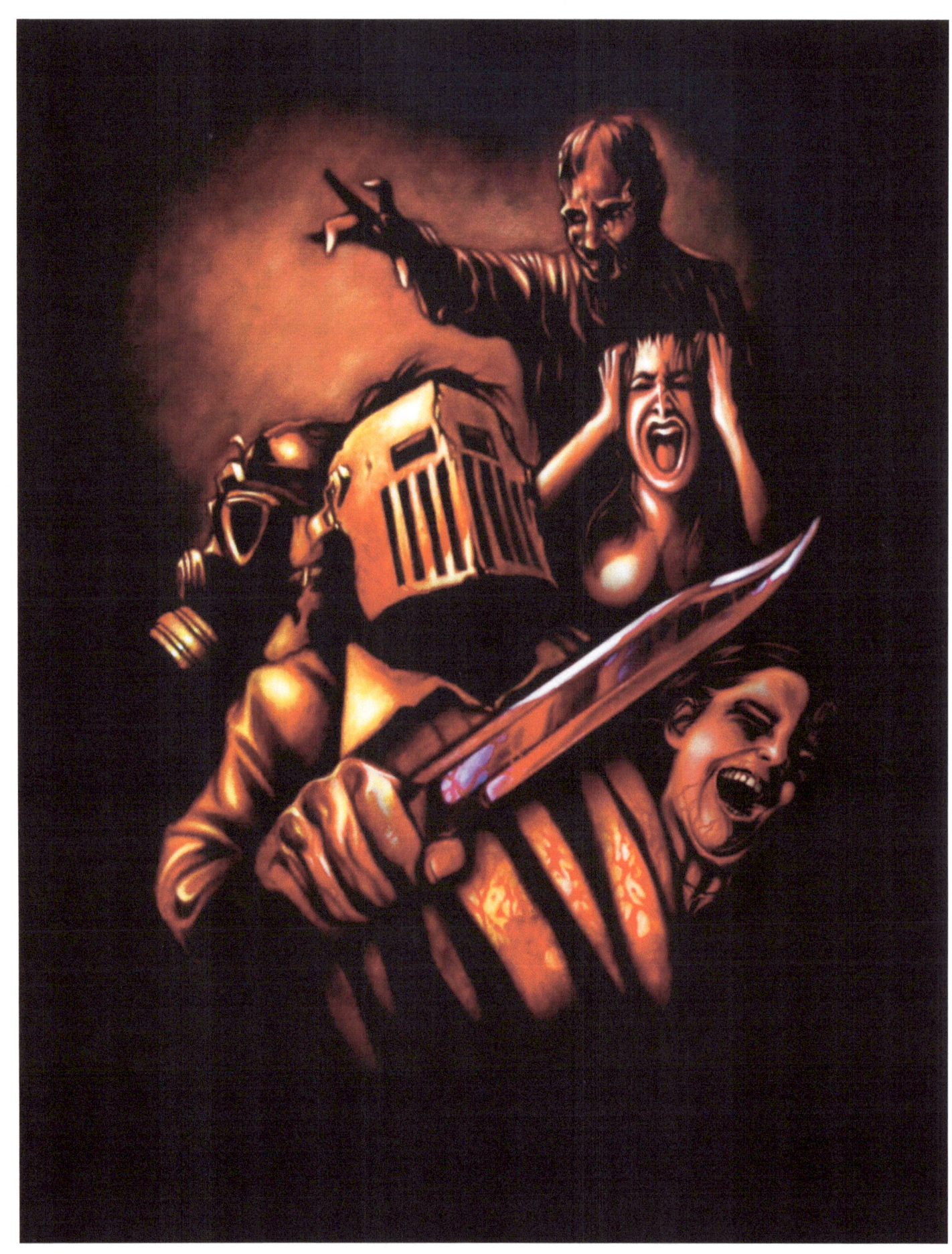

Violent Shit
DVD Cover for Synapse Films

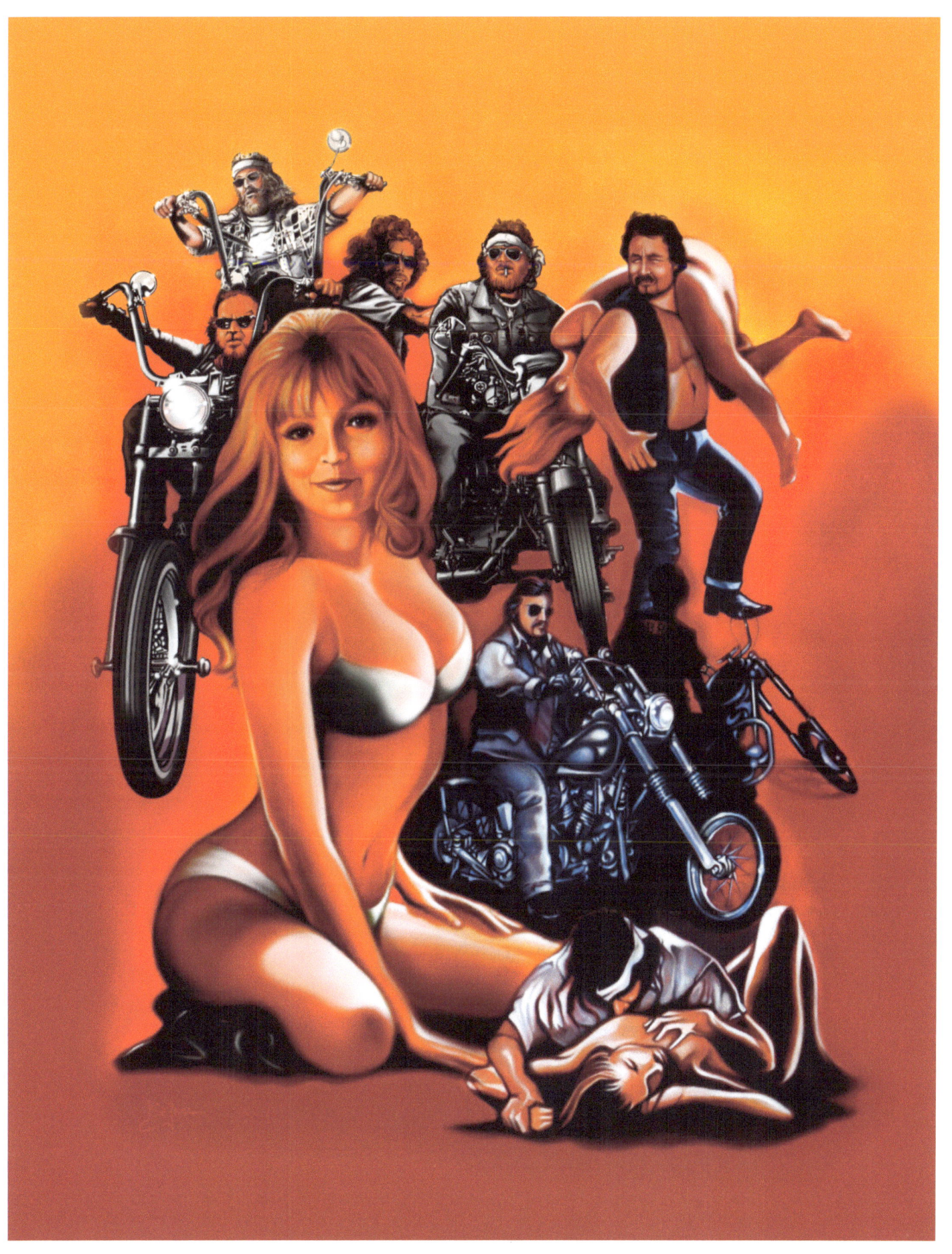

Bad Bad Gang!
DVD Cover for Synapse Films

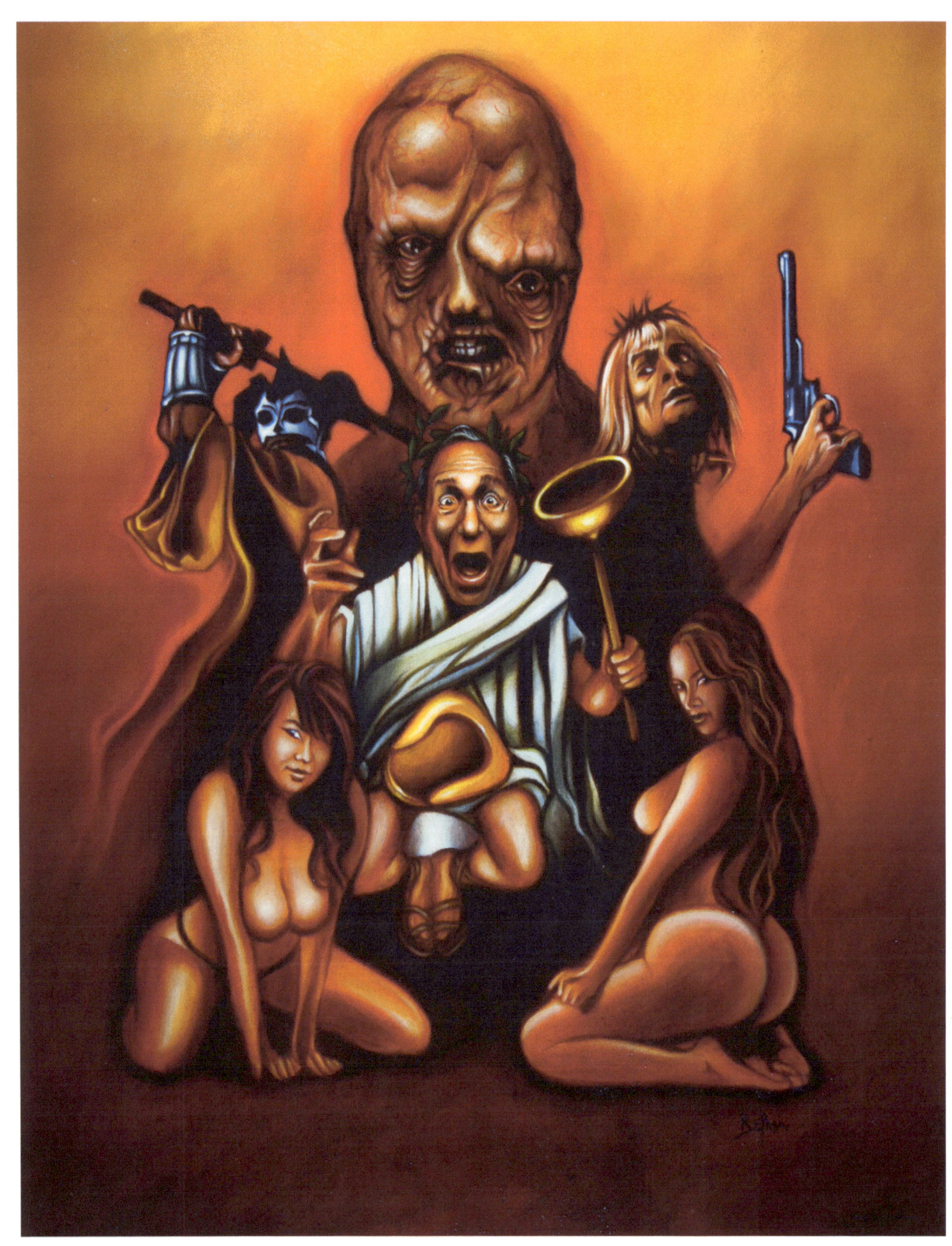

Troma Films

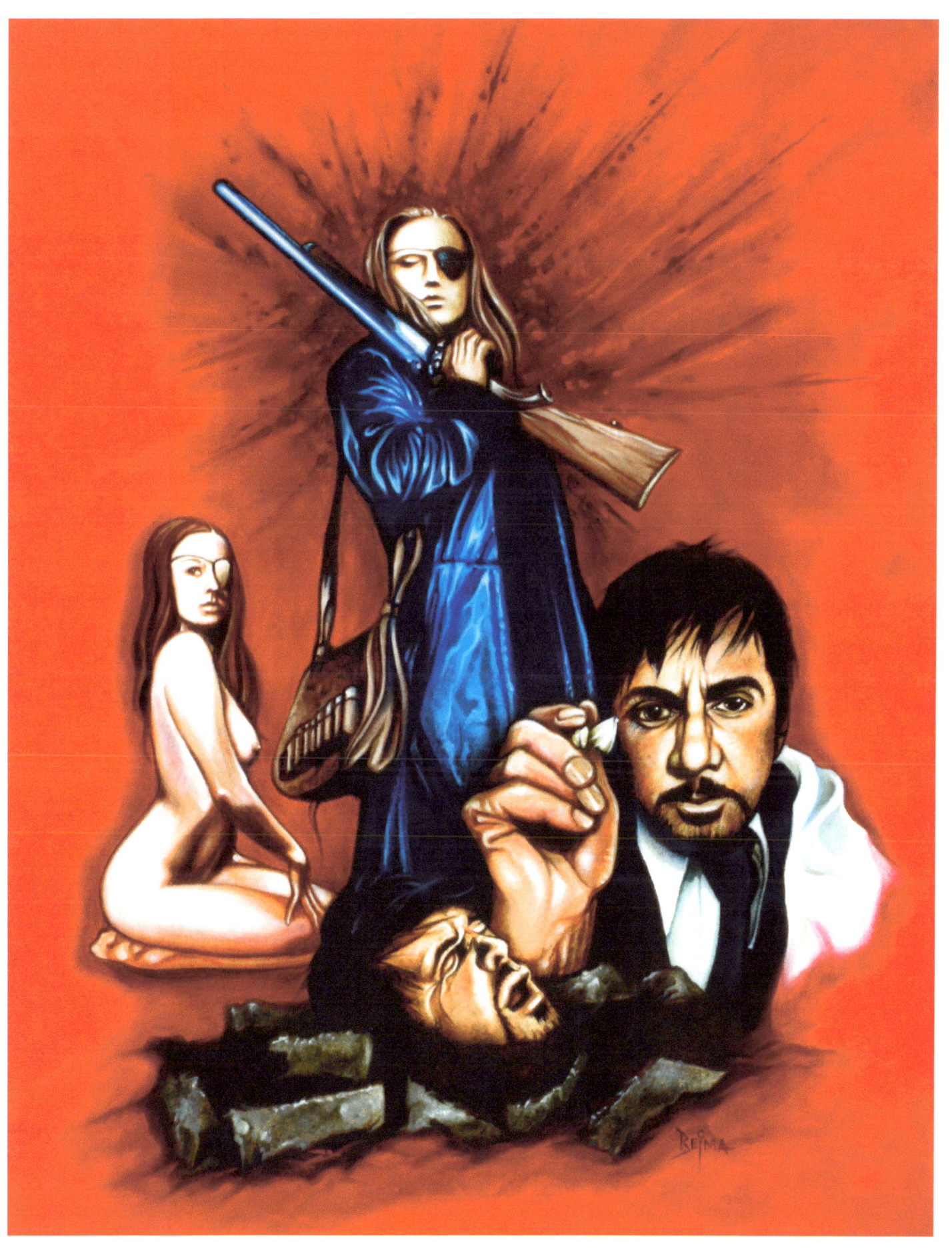

Thriller
For Synapse Films

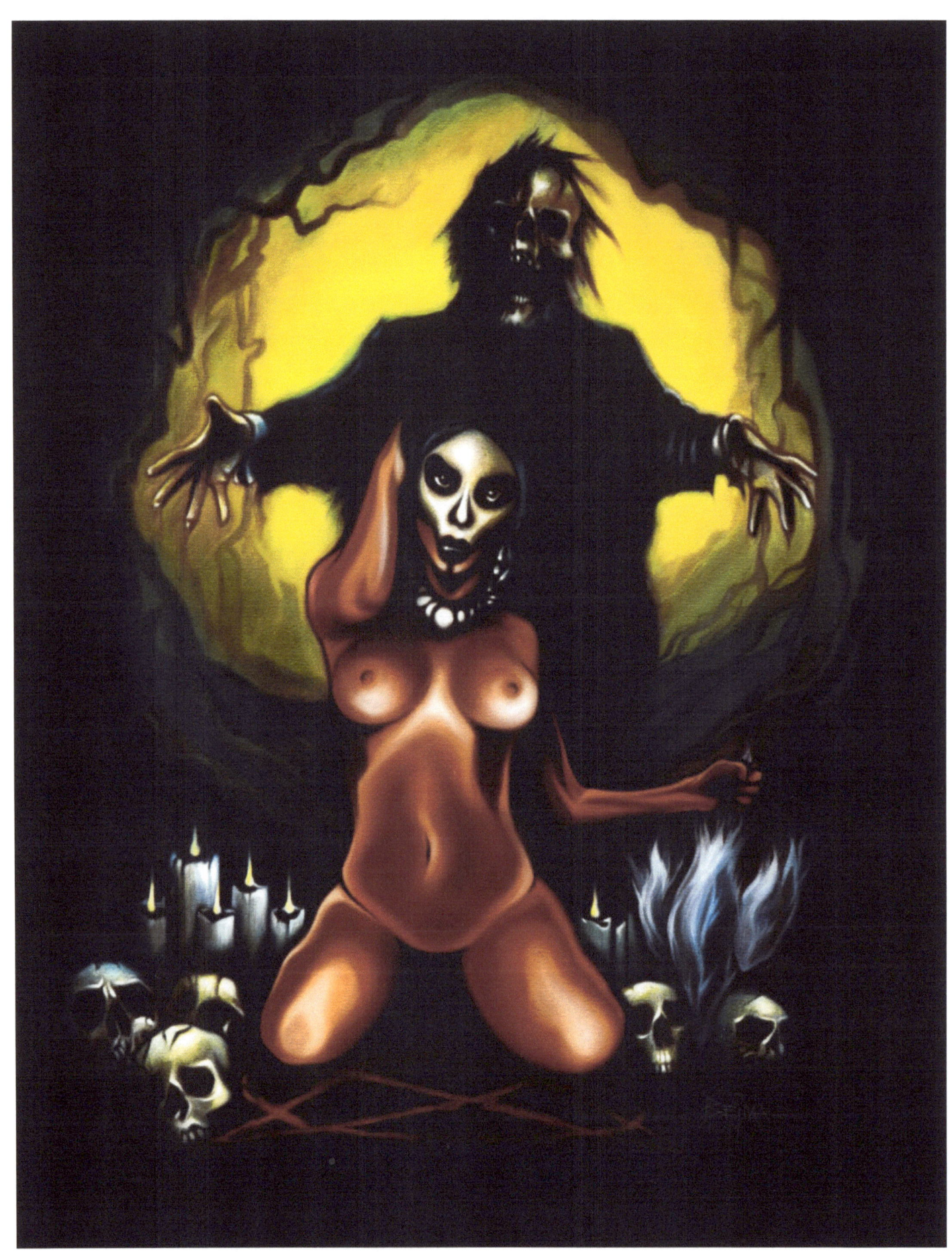

Recurring Nightmares
for Great Lakes Association of Horror Writers

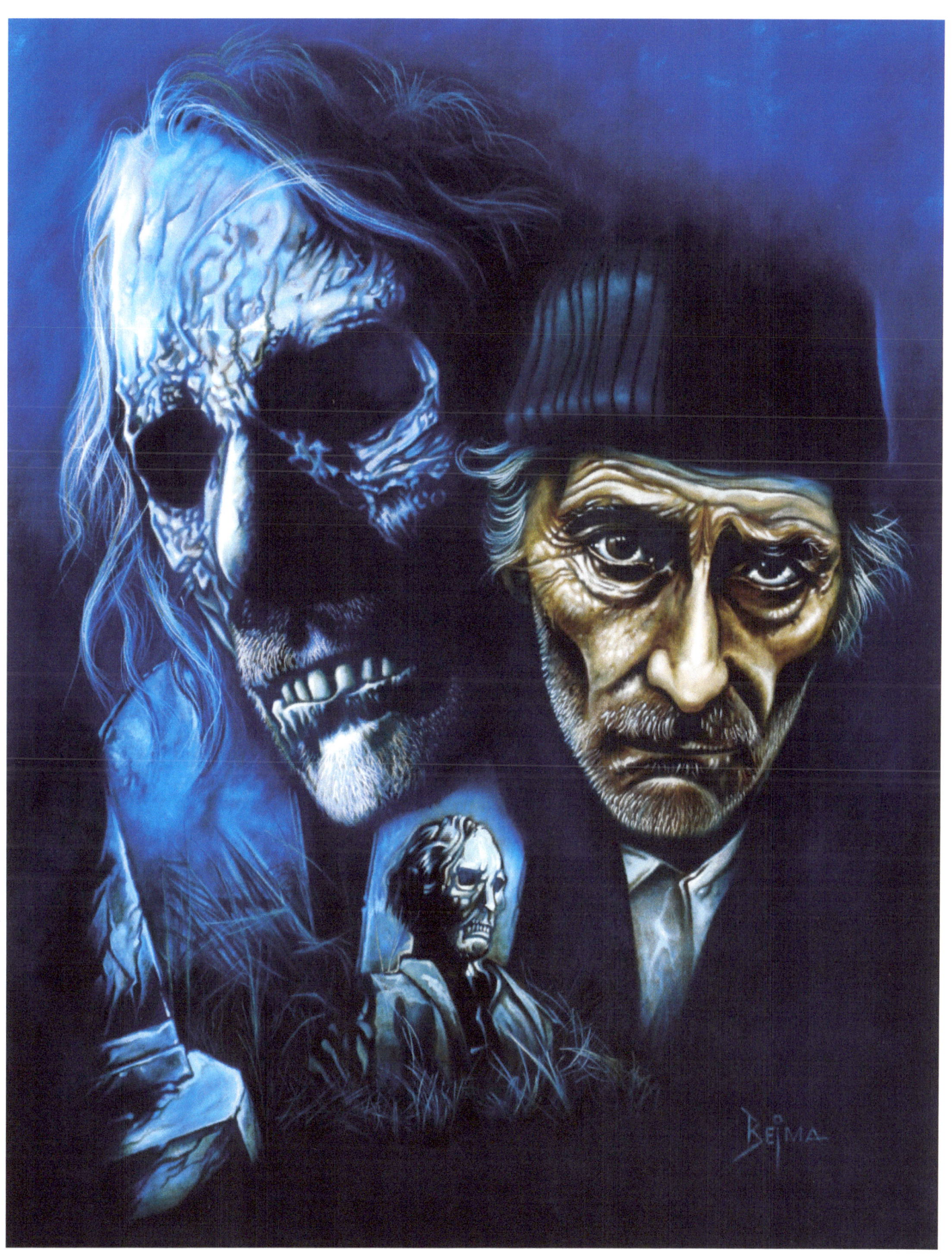

Tales From the Crypt

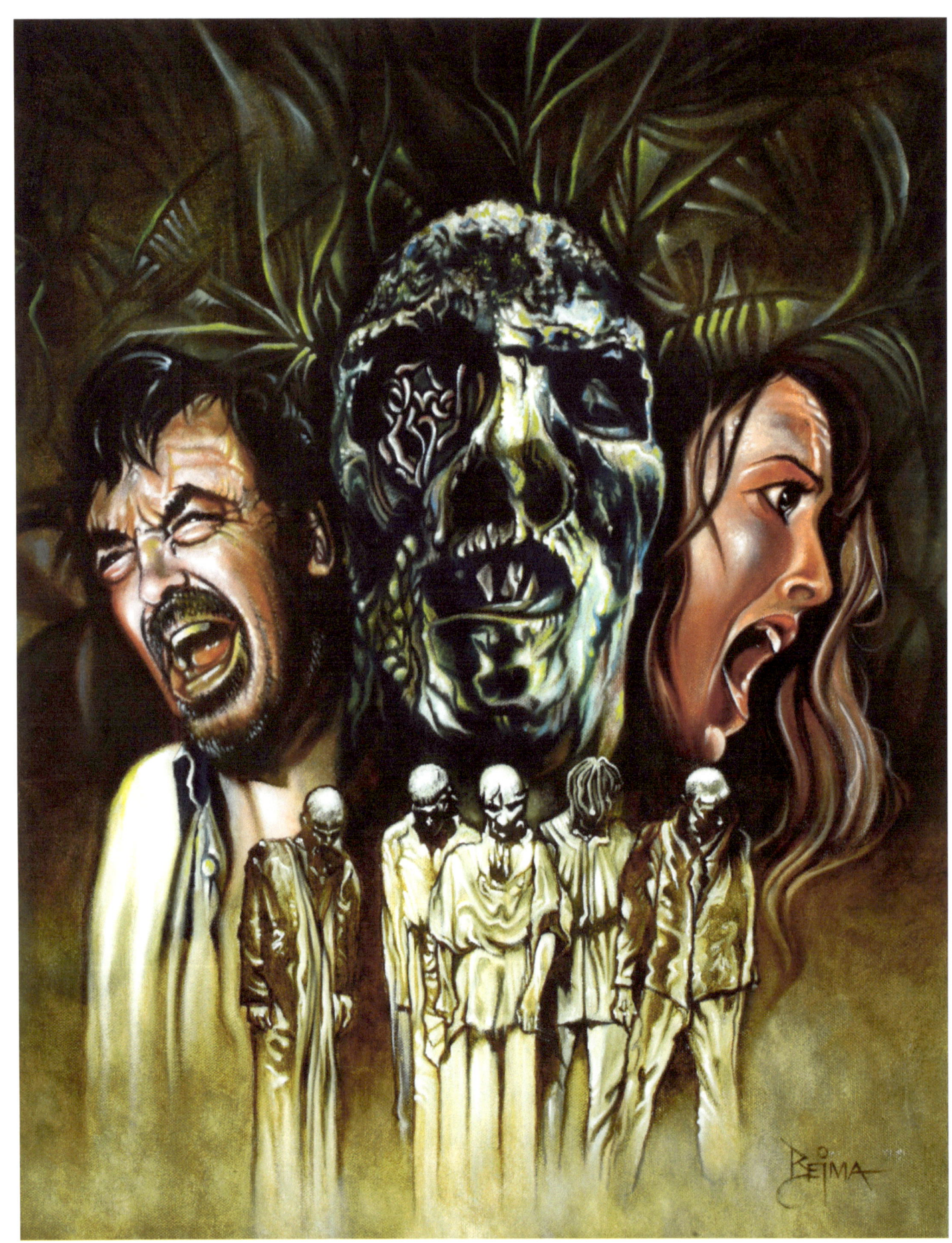

Zombie II

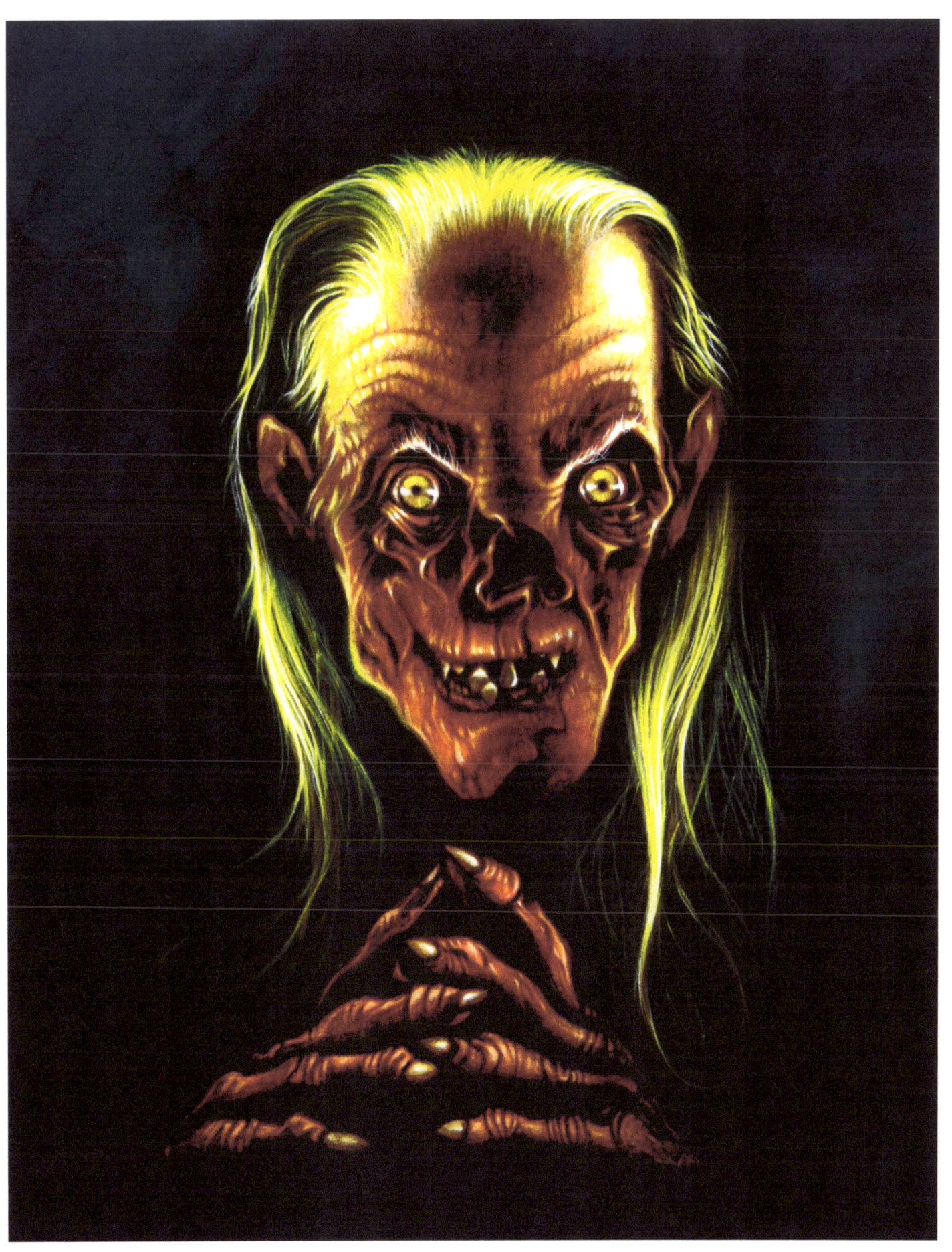

Tales From the Crypt

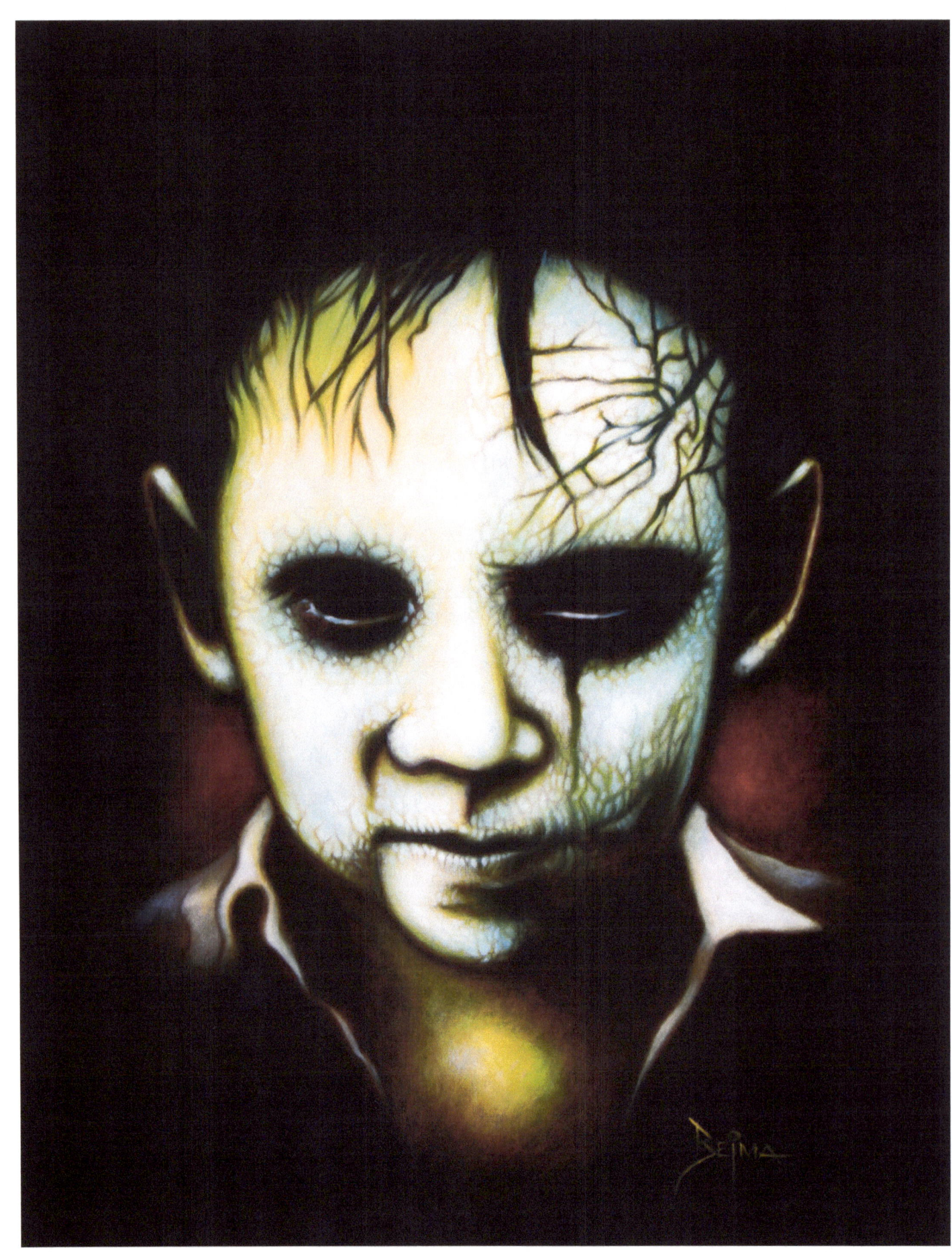

The Devil's Backbone

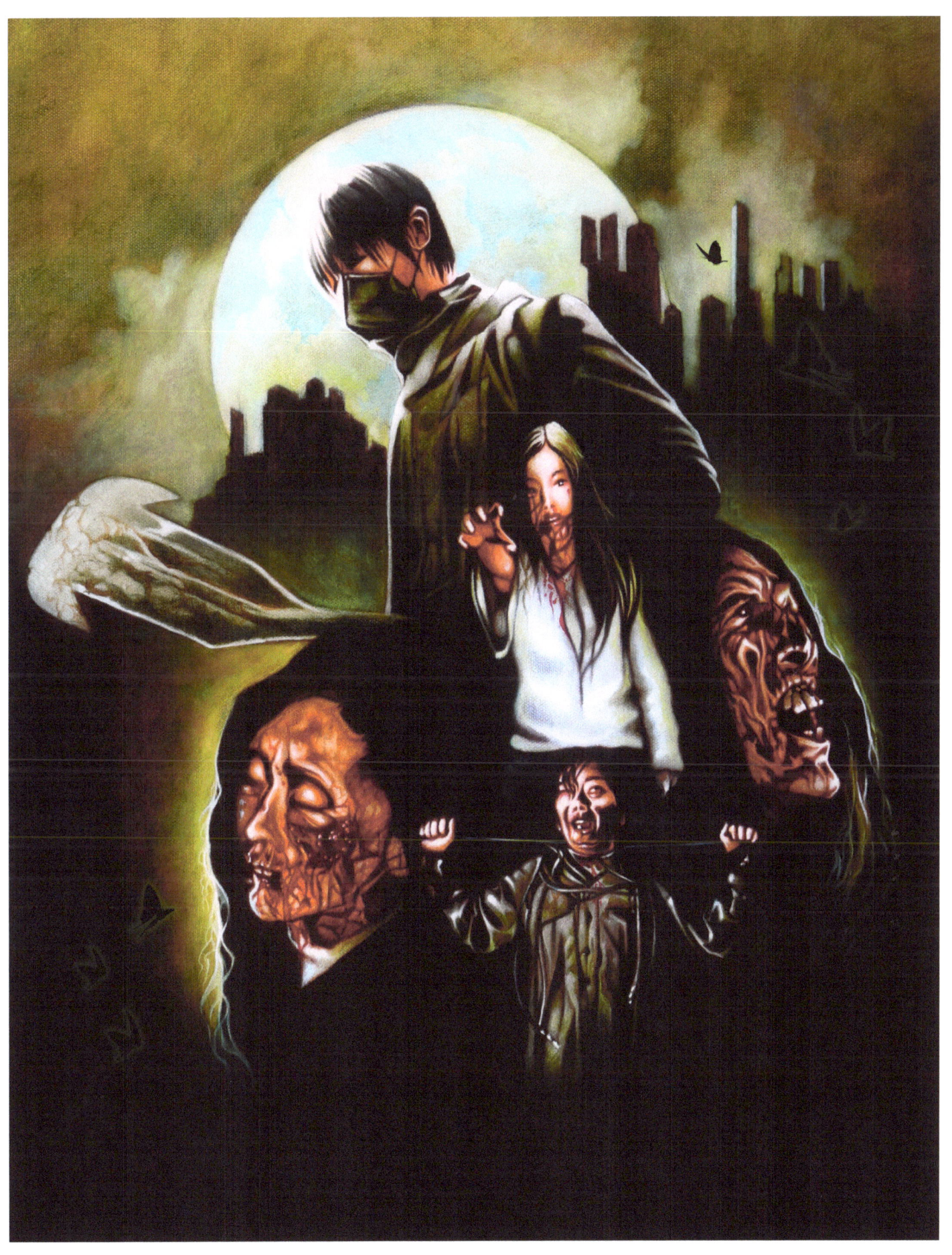

Undertaker
DVD Cover For Synapse Films

COLLECT THE WHOLE
MASTERS OF THE DARK ART SERIES AT
www.ASYLUMPUBLICATIONS.com

All characters and titles not in the public domain remain protected pursuant to the copyright owners or claimants of the respective studios, production companies, filmmakers, authors, or other rights holders, if applicable. The inclusion herein of such characters and titles is strictly for journalistic and/or informational commentary or scholarly review and use of the same is in no way intended to imply transfer, authorization, ownership, or other claimant rights other than for such use.

www.ingramcontent.com/pod-product-compliance
Lightning Source LLC
Chambersburg PA
CBHW040455220526
45473CB00004B/1642